FINDING HIS FOOTPRINTS *in the* SAND

Using a woman named Erica Kim, God has spoken to my own woman's heart about His unconditional love and acceptance for me. Oh, I know about that love and acceptance—have known it and experienced it for years. But *Footprints in the Sand* is an emotional and visual reminder of this great truth, taking it deeper into the reader's heart, where it can "become flesh" and change the way we think and live. This is a powerful study for women at any stage of their walk with Christ. Highly recommended!

—**Kathi Macias**, award-winning author of more than 40 books, including *Mothers of the Bible Speak to Mothers of Today.*

Mrs. Kim correctly zeroes in on grace as the foundational basis and sustaining power in our relationship with God. With each scriptural example, she moves the reader off a treadmill of performance and onto the freedom of living under the warm glow of unmerited favor. *Finding His Footprints in the Sand* offers hope to anyone that struggles with being "good enough" for God.

—**Julie Zine Coleman**, author of *Unexpected Love: God's Heart Revealed through Jesus' Conversations with Women,* Thomas Nelson, 2013.

FINDING HIS FOOTPRINTS *in the* SAND

God's Grace to
WOMEN *in an*
Ungracious World

ERICA S. KIM

NEW YORK

FINDING HIS FOOTPRINTS *in the* SAND
God's Grace to WOMEN *in an Ungracious World*

Published in New York, New York, by Morgan James Publishing. Morgan James and The Entrepreneurial Publisher are trademarks of Morgan James, LLC. www.MorganJamesPublishing.com

The Morgan James Speakers Group can bring authors to your live event. For more information or to book an event visit The Morgan James Speakers Group at www.TheMorganJamesSpeakersGroup.com.

A **free** eBook edition is available with the purchase of this print book.

CLEARLY PRINT YOUR NAME ABOVE IN UPPER CASE

Instructions to claim your free eBook edition:
1. Download the BitLit app for Android or iOS
2. Write your name in **UPPER CASE** on the line
3. Use the BitLit app to submit a photo
4. Download your eBook to any device

ISBN 978-1-63047-431-7 paperback
ISBN 978-1-63047-432-4 eBook
ISBN 978-1-63047-433-1 hardcover
Library of Congress Control Number:
2014915925

Cover Design by:
Rachel Lopez
www.r2cdesign.com

Interior Design by:
Bonnie Bushman
bonnie@caboodlegraphics.com

In an effort to support local communities, raise awareness and funds, Morgan James Publishing donates a percentage of all book sales for the life of each book to Habitat for Humanity Peninsula and Greater Williamsburg.

Get involved today, visit
www.MorganJamesBuilds.com

Habitat
for Humanity®
Peninsula and
Greater Williamsburg
Building Partner

DEDICATION

To my husband, Frank, and to my girls and their husbands
who are the greatest confirmation of God's grace in my life.

TABLE OF CONTENTS

FOREWORD

For years, I have known and respected Erica from afar. I watched as she began her Christian life, first as a college student, and then as a young wife, then as a young mother of three beautiful daughters, and finally, as she and Frank served on the mission field in Japan. I witnessed from afar her courage and faithfulness when she went through the death of her mother and, and later, when she battled Lupus. There are things we admire in people from a distance - perhaps when they don't even know we are watching - as they go through the ups and downs of life and remain devoted, faithful and courageous. In that way, I admired and respected Erica for a long time. However, in recent years, I have been blessed to know Erica as a friend, and I have come to respect her even more. She is a woman who loves deeply and gives of herself completely. Her faith and convictions become only more obvious as you get closer. And that is what I love about her book...

In this book, Erica lets us into her heart and allows us to know her. She allows us to walk with her as she learns to trust and embrace God's love and grace in the midst of, in spite of, and even *because* of, incredible challenges.

Like many of us, Erica struggled with accepting God's grace and love. Through these pages, Erica shares her personal challenges and victories in her journey to better comprehend the depth of God's mercy and compassion amidst tragedy, sickness and loss of loved ones. Along with stories from her life, she uses the Scriptures to carry us with her to a deeper appreciation of God's wonderful love, hope, joy and peace.

This book is full of vulnerability, faith, human examples and priceless nuggets of wisdom that will remain with you long after you have finished reading it. I think Paul described best what Erica has so beautifully been able to do for us:

Praise be to the God and Father of our Lord Jesus Christ, the Father of compassion and the God of all comfort, who comforts us in all our troubles, so that we can comfort those in any trouble with the comfort we ourselves receive from God. For just as we share abundantly in the sufferings of Christ, so also our comfort abounds through Christ.

(II Corinthians 1: 3-5, NIV)

—**Geri Laing**, Women's Ministry Leader and Elder's Wife for the South Florida Church of Christ

ACKNOWLEDGEMENTS

This book could not have been possible without the help of so many people who took out the time to read, to edit and to comment on all the different aspects of this book. With any book, it takes a team of dedicated individuals who care and who are concerned enough to take a set of ideas and help build it into a tangible and cohesive book. I would like to thank each of those special friends, family and partners in the faith who sacrificed so much of their time and energy to help me bring this project together.

I would like to thank my agent, Steve, who spent hours and hours working with me on the manuscript and for believing in me. I am so grateful to those who read, critiqued and edited the manuscript when it was still in its initial form. Thank you Janet, Dawn, Geri, Miyoko, Manami, Debbie, Beth and others who took out time to read, comment and edit the manuscript when it was still its early stages. Your encouragement and support was invaluable.

Most of all I want to thank my husband, Frank, who helped me through the emotions as well as through all the writings. He went through every single word to edit them exactly as he knew I felt them. I appreciate the months and hours of time after work he put into this. Without him, I could not have put this all together and done it with the accuracy that it deserved. Thank you honey! You are the best!

Introduction

THIS UNGRACIOUS WORLD

On February 8, 1988 while living in San Francisco, I received a phone call from my father, who was living in New Jersey at the time. "Your mother killed herself. I found her dead today," he said in almost a whisper. As soon as he finished his sentence, I crumpled to the kitchen floor. I wailed so loudly that my 15-month-old baby, Miyoko, who had been playing in her room, came running and began to stroke my head as if I was the baby, and not her. Cradling the phone that was attached to the wall, my body heaved as I wept and wept. After a few minutes passed, my father said, "Come home." What came out of my mouth following his words surprised me. "It's your fault," I replied while weeping. "Did you hear me? You did this to her." The phone clicked as my father hung up.

In my grief and pain, I blamed my father. I was alone with my daughter and held her as I continued to cry for another hour before picking up the phone to leave a message for my husband who had flown to Japan early that morning. My mind raced in different directions. I was four months pregnant with our second child and had been frantically trying to contact my mother all day, since I had begun to spot that morning. My mother was a nurse, so I wanted her advice. The next day, in spite of being in a fog of grief, I made an emergency appointment to see my obstetrician. During my appointment, the doctor told me that if I got on a plane, I would probably lose the baby. I didn't care anymore. I wanted to go home.

Many of us have experienced tragedy, abuse, and different forms of suffering, often in ways that are unique to us as women. God looks at each of us and knows our pain and feels each one of those scars. Even though we are Christians, when faced with crisis, our first response is too often not one of grace but rather a desire to lash out and blame others. Other times, we run away, withdrawing from even those who love us most. It is during these kinds of times that we see how much grace we lack in our lives and how much more we need to understand it, both for ourselves and towards others.

Jesus never lashed out from the cross. He endured a deep agony that we may never have to undergo during our lifetime just so we would not have to suffer eternally. It is through his life and attitude that we are taught how to respond in the most difficult times. Even though my general nature is to be easily forgiving towards others, I was not prepared for my response in times of grief. I saw that my faith and my heart were not strong enough to endure and to respond with the kind of grace that Jesus had shown me. I fell short with my father who was already torn up by his own feelings of guilt. I reacted badly toward him and toward others during that time in my life.

The reality is that we live in an ungracious world. For this reason, our upbringing and our past experiences have imprinted certain reactions and natural responses in each one of us. We often respond in ways that we have seen others do. It is said that most of us have lived with some type of dysfunctionality in our upbringing. Those memories can impact us more than God's love and grace. Our emotional scars can cause us to be insecure and often give us a warped or incomplete perception of grace, despite the fact that we are Christians.

This was my experience.

Even though I had been a Christian and worked in Christian ministry, my view of myself and of my relationship with God was somewhat distorted, and this influenced how I saw God's grace. After becoming a Christian, I believed that God forgave me, but I often did not *feel* forgiven when I sinned. Intellectually, I knew that I was saved, but I would often doubt my salvation depending on my mood and emotions. I had faith in the Bible as the true Word of God, and I was encouraged by the promises of God, but I did not always trust that they would hold firm for *me* and *my* life. Eventually, I had to confront the fact that not understanding God's promised grace was crippling me.

Because of our experiences in this fallen world, God's grace can often take a back seat in our motivation, our faith and our self-esteem. Ungraciousness has given birth to bitterness, unforgiveness, resentment and anger. Who can count the friendships, marriages, and families that have been torn apart by a lack of grace?

Grace was meant to teach us to say "no" to the graceless influences of this world—not just in our actions, but also in our thoughts. *For the grace of God has appeared that offers salvation to all people. It teaches us to say "No" to ungodliness and worldly passions, and to live self-controlled, upright and godly lives in this present age.* (Titus 2:12, NIV) Grace was intended to demonstrate God's love for us, providing us with confidence in our relationship with Him. It was the ultimate expression of his affection for each of us. Grace is what makes us, not just friends, but children of God.

> *How great is the love the Father has lavished on us, that we should be called children of God! And that is what we are! The reason the world does not know us is that it did not know him. Dear friends, now we are children of God, and what we will be has not yet been made known. But we know that when he appears we shall be like him, for we shall see him as he is. Everyone who has this hope in him purifies himself, just as he is pure.*
>
> (1 John 3:1-3, NIV)

We have a great hope knowing that God loves us. The scripture above tells us that when we realize how he has lavished us with love and put our hope in him, we are purified just as he is pure. Yet, even this gift of grace from God and the blood of Christ do not instantly change our thinking from the way we were raised. From the early years of my life, I saw all kinds of abuse, drug addiction, alcoholism, greed and adultery around me. My cultural background as a Japanese forced me to maintain an exterior that hid these awful truths, giving others the impression that my family was "perfect." Our external façade had a bright neon sign saying, "Success, Riches and the American Dream."

Imperfection would have shamed my family, and I felt obligated to maintain the family's honor. Later, even after converting from Buddhism to Christianity in my teenage years, I still struggled with the patterns of my upbringing. I was living out my Christianity with the same set of paradigms that I had grown up with. Satan began to create the perfect storm, beginning with my mother's death, which uncovered some of the deeper layers of my broken past where scars, fears and mistrust existed in my heart. None of this takes away from the fact that I love my family and feel a deep gratitude towards them.

Like me, no one understands grace fully at the time of his or her conversion. Fully realizing God's grace is a life-long journey that we must experience in our spiritual walk with the Lord. I have counseled women for nearly thirty years on three different continents and in many different cities. I see a common thread that links every one of us: we all need God's grace in our lives. Many of us carry emotional and, in some cases, physical scars. Trauma and suffering can bring out these scars and the hurt can be profound. We, women, feel deeply and thus are easily shaken through such difficulties.

After more than thirty years in Christ, I am still far from being perfect. I need continual reassurance from God to know that he still loves me and keeps forgiving me. At the same time, I can now see more clearly how he has truly lavished me with abundant grace. And I am confident that He has done the same for you too. I hope that through these pages, you will discover more of his grace in your life, and you will see how his grace has led you safe thus far and how it will truly lead you home.

Chapter 1

FOR GOD
SO LOVED THE WORLD

"For God so loved the world that he gave his only Son, so that everyone who believes in him may not perish but may have eternal life."

(John 3:16 NRSV)

God Loves Us So Much

God had a defining moment—he loved us so much that he gave his one and only Son to die on the cross for us. This was the culmination of God's love for us and became the event that would change all of mankind for eternity. He loved us when we were sinners. He loved us when we ignored him. He loved us when we were good. He loved us when we were evil. He loved us even when Satan had total control over our lives. There is nothing in all of creation that can separate us from God's love (Romans 8:38-39).

I had a defining moment. My mother had been suicidal for many years, but she had made a promise to me that she would never truly go through with it. I thought that she loved me so much that she would never actually take her own life. I trusted that she would live for my brother and me no matter how hard her life became. When my father called me with the horrible news, I was stunned. My mother had broken her promise, and her action proved to me that "she didn't love me anymore". This thought spiraled into: If my own mother doesn't love me enough to live, then how could God love me?

Though this correlation may not make sense to some who are reading this, it was a logical thought-process for me at the time. From that time on, my mother's death became an incorrect focal point in my understanding of God's grace. Based on this experience, I fabricated a false set of principles in my heart that Satan exploited. He threw one stone at a time, month after month, year after year, to assault my walk with God, crippling my faith and nearly destroying me spiritually over the next several years.

On February 9, 1988, after my doctor's appointment and against his professional advice, I flew home. I was intent on being at my mother's wake and funeral service. However, the following day, I ended up missing the wake because of heavy cramping and bleeding which eventually led to a miscarriage. Just as my doctor had predicted, I lay in bed with intense pain, while a friend sat by me for several hours as everyone else left to attend the wake. Before everyone came home, I had lost the baby. I attended the funeral service the next day, acted as if nothing had happened and delivered a eulogy for my mother. For appearance's sake, I hardened my heart to the growing pain that was crushing me from the inside out.

The worst part of all of this was that my mother had been out to visit me in San Francisco earlier that week, and she had left the day before her suicide. I played reruns in my mind: all the things I had said or didn't say to her as well as all the things I did or didn't do for her during her visit. Unfortunately, my mind convinced me that I fell short in every area and that somehow, I had contributed to the cause of her death. Here I was in the Christian ministry, and I couldn't even help my own mother. A tumor of doubt and mistrust took root deep inside my heart that prevented me from experiencing the full extent of God's graciousness. The scene had been set for Satan.

I have heard that there is often guilt or regret after experiencing the death of a close relative or friend. My mother's suicide left me drowning in so much guilt that it was strangling me inside. I tried to talk to people about how I felt about my losses, but was often met with well-intentioned but unsatisfying answers such as:

"You need to trust God."

"God works out everything for the good."

There were also some hurtful statements like:

"Everyone dies sometime. Your mother just decided to make it happen sooner, and your baby might have been born with a defect if you didn't miscarry."

"Your mother was selfish. How could she do that to your family?"

Such attempts to "reassure" me caused me to clam up for many years. I chose to mask my sorrow with hard work and drove myself so intensely that my health would breakdown on many days. I wanted to block out the pain by "pleasing" God with good behavior and hard toil for the ministry.

Somewhere deep inside my heart, I also blamed myself for my mother's death. If I had just tried harder, she wouldn't have died. If I had told her how important she was to me, she would have not killed herself. It was all about *my* efforts. From that incident, I would never let *my* lack of effort hurt anyone else in my life including God. So in every area, I pushed myself beyond what was healthy. I worked into the middle of the night and woke up extremely early for the next few years. I prayed for hours each week. I read my Bible for at least an hour a day. All good deeds—but I wasn't experiencing the healing I needed.

I wanted to "earn" God's acceptance and blessing. I wanted to be "good enough" for God to bless the rest of my life. As a result, just a few years after my mother's death, I was diagnosed with a disease called SLE or Systemic Lupus Erythematosus, an autoimmune disease that can affect nearly every part of the body, including the skin, joints, lungs, heart, kidneys, brain, and blood. Obviously, I was no longer able to cover the pain in my heart with "good works," nor was I able to be "what God wanted me to be" in my spiritual life or my job. In the end, I began to believe that God did not want to use me anymore, because I was just not good enough. I had no personal successes to speak of—instead, I was sick, bedridden, and convinced that I was a useless wretch. I was in desperate need of grace.

God's Grace in the Old and New Testaments

When I used to think about God's grace, I never considered the richness and depth of its many aspects and characteristics. In fact, I saw grace primarily as a concept found only in the New Testament. However, as I have studied the Bible, I have seen his divine grace in both the Old and New Testaments.

In the Old Testament, the Hebrew word *chesed* is used, which William Tyndale translated as loving-kindness. The Hebrew Bible also uses the word *hanam,* which means spontaneous gift of affection or unmerited favor and *raham* which means mercy and compassion, a definition also implying that the relationship was broken but mended by mercy. The New Testament uses the Greek word *charis,* which literally means "gift." Taking all these meanings together, we can say that God's grace is a gift of loving-kindness and unmerited favor mending a broken relationship.

Who broke this relationship? All of us did (Romans 3:23). But God mended it, healed it and now, nurtures it. He made our wrecked relationship whole again, and he continues to do this day after day. Through his relationship with us, he takes our broken lives and restores us. He nurses our bruised souls back to health. He takes our lost dreams and gives us new ones. Through reconciling with us, he makes us whole again and again.

And again.

This is his special *charis* or gift to each of us.

I needed healing from disappointments and tragedy. My physical health was broken. But more than that, I had a bruised soul that I couldn't believe would ever be nursed back to health. I had become trapped in my old pattern of relying on all my "good works" to maintain a worthy standing with God. Instead of changing my heart, I just pushed myself harder, and it wasn't working. And yet, through it all, God's grace was present.

He is Always There

God had revealed his grace over and over to me, but my eyes were blinded by my tarnished set of glasses, which distorted how I viewed the hurtful events in my life. Those same experiences also tainted how I saw God's Word. My preconceptions distorted how I interpreted and digested the definition of grace, an astonishingly beautiful, all-embracing and wonderful message, which I had shrunk down to the limits of my inadequate works and deeds.

Part of God's grace means that even when we are weak and fallen, God's power is made perfect (2 Corinthians 12:9-10). He patiently guards our salvation even as we struggle with our shortcomings.

In the midst of our darkness, when we put up walls and try our best to protect ourselves, we don't realize how his gracious hand is holding us, sustaining us and comforting us. During the times when we are angry and feel all alone, God holds us tightly, never letting go as we sit in hopelessness. Though we block out his words and stop listening, he tenderly whispers into our ears as we weep into a pillow wet with our sorrows. He dries our tears with the soft and compassionate caress of his hands that we didn't believe were there anymore. Even as we turn our face away from him, he holds us close to his heart. We may not see it; we may not feel it, but God's grace is always there.

Finding Treasure

Treasures are often found in dark places.

> And I will give you treasures hidden in the darkness—**secret riches**.

> I will do this so you may know that I am the Lord, the God of Israel, the one who calls you by name.
>
> (Isaiah 45:3 NLT)

No one hides a treasure where it is visible for all to see; rather it is strategically hidden so that only the one who is willing to persevere and to make sacrifices can find the fortune. Many are the tales of rich treasure hidden away somewhere deep under the ground or in the depths of the ocean. In the same way, just like Christ had to face deep darkness to come into his glory, so we, too, must go into dark places to find the spiritual treasures that await us.

I did not realize that the treasures God wanted to give me were hidden in *darkness*. I had to go to dark places—through dark times—to see his grace more clearly and plainly. Those tragic events didn't feel like love at the time. In fact, they felt like punishment and rejection for wrongs I had done. I secretly stopped believing in God's goodness in *my* life. Behind closed doors, his promises did not work for me but only in others who were more *worthy.* God had promised me many blessings, but I was furtively cynical and doubtful.

I finally decided to take off my distorted glasses when I reread the Bible's many scriptures on grace. God had revealed his grace over and over to me, but my eyes were blinded by hurtful events in my life. Those same experiences also tainted how I saw God's Word. My preconceptions controlled how I interpreted and digested the definition of grace, an astonishingly all-embracing and wonderful message, which I had shrunk down to my inadequate works and deeds. The power of my destructive thinking likewise cloaked the beauty of his grace, because my mind contained so many personal prejudices and presuppositions. Ultimately, I discovered that God's love was far-reaching, and greatly beyond what I had originally imagined

I also realized that God loved women in a very special way—with a graciousness encompassed by gentleness and empathy. Slowly, and ever so surely, this deepened understanding of God's true grace began to transform my attitude and my walk with the Lord.

Defined By the Master
(Suggested Reading: Psalm 139)
When I was young, my mother made Japanese flower arrangements. They were so skillfully done that yearly she was invited to display her work in the special exhibition space on the top-floor lobby of what used to be the World Trade Center in New York City. Every year, she spent weeks planning out her designs before each show, taking great care to make each floral presentation perfect. Sometimes, she used branches with only one flower stem. Other times, she used several kinds of flowers and interspersed them with tree branches, always keeping them simple and never overly decorated or ostentatious. The simplicity of her designs brought out a beauty in the flowers that made the displays appealing to the eye.

I would attend all these exhibitions with enthusiasm. Among all the presentations, I was always most impressed with my mother's display, not because it had the most flowers, but because of the meticulous harmony within each piece—flowers, branches and leaves arranged to perfection. She would often use uncommon flowers and branches, those that most might consider to be weeds or useless twigs. My mother's designs were often praised and given awards. She was so proud of her arrangements. Her gift to see beauty in simplicity made her work flawless in expressing the true peace and balance of what the Japanese call *Ikebana* or the art of floral arrangement.

In a similar way, God created women special. He defined us with unique qualities, making each one of us a special masterpiece. Much like flowers, all women are beautiful. Every minute detail—some simple, some more complicated—perfectly balanced in harmony to make us who we are. God considered every feature and attribute and designed us to be fearfully and wonderfully made (Psalm 139:14). He fashioned each one of us to be attractive and alluring. Each of us possesses a unique blend of beauty, color and fragrance. Whether you feel beautiful or not, God made you pleasing and appealing to others, including the opposite sex. Even our voices are, on average, an octave higher than men's voices. The same voice can arouse emotions and calm children. God delighted in creating you exactly as you are.

Often, we look at ourselves in the mirror...and we don't see a flower but rather a weed. We look at our legs and see redwood trunks rather than willowy flower stems. We gaze down at our bodies and see giant mushrooms rather than God's magnificent handiwork.

Take another look.

No, those large hips were not a mistake. No, that bump on your nose was no slip-up. No, that little bulge in your mid-section was not an oversight. No, those bushy eyebrows were not a blunder. What we may perceive as imperfections in ourselves are not flaws at all. They are ingredients for a work of art, shaped by the master himself.

God created us as extraordinary beings. He personally designed each of us to be a spectacular and *unique* arrangement of intellect, emotion, physique, and spirit. Most amazingly, we are each a reflection of him.

Designed by His Grace

When we recognize God's supreme wisdom and decide to acknowledge and accept his unparalleled discernment, it is easier to embrace every wrinkle, birthmark, bulge and blemish—whether physical or deep within our character—as a part of God's greater plan to help us to know and to understand him better. Even those aspects of ourselves that we may loathe or consider inconvenient were actually crafted by our Maker with precision and with deep love. Those sometimes frustrating qualities have a purpose. They help us to understand how much we need him, and they fan the desire to have a relationship with him throughout our whole lifetime.

The blemishes are there for a reason too. No one is perfect. No one is without limitations. No one is without problems. Yet, it is often precisely because of these "failings" that we discover the *love that never fails*. It is when we feel worthless that we might humbly realize that His grace redefines us as being incredibly full of worth. If we never felt weak, we might have never turn to our Creator for strength and, most of all, for salvation.

Some of us may look at our frailties and imperfections and ask: *Why should I try to change and get rid of my shortcomings, if this is the way God made me? I hate my sinful nature, but why do I get blamed for it?*

God answers us through the scriptures:

> *"So one of you will ask me: "Then why does God blame us for our sins? Who can fight his will?" You are only human, and human beings have no right to question God. An object should not ask the person who made it, "Why did you make me like this?" The potter can make anything he wants to make. He can use the same clay to make one thing for special use and another thing for daily use.*
>
> (Romans 9:19-21 NCV)

We can either blame God or thank him for who we are. I used to look at all my faults and become frustrated with myself. Then, it suddenly struck me that my shortcomings are what compel me to get down on my knees every day. Those weaknesses keep me relying on God every day of my life. So now, I can be grateful for who I am before God, warts and all! I wake up in the morning and feel thankful for how he made me. I can even laugh about many of my frailties (though they might not be funny at times for others). I no longer have to get down on myself, but strive to repent when my sinful nature takes over. Concurrently, I constantly work through the power of the

Holy Spirit to help me produce the fruits of the Spirit as I pray to conquer my temptations and inadequacies.

When we are truly grateful for God's grace, we learn to accept who we are and how we have been created in his sight. The people who live with this kind of appreciation have a joy and enthusiasm that seem to ooze out of them. Their faith is contagious and full of fresh hope. They are vibrant in their demeanors and are able to pour out love to all those around them, because they are not focused on themselves. Their thankfulness is genuine, and it endures through the tough times without failing to produce joy in others as well.

Defined by Grace

We do not have to define ourselves by how others see us or treat us or even by how we see ourselves. Often, we compare ourselves to others and desperately fall short. Other times, we can look at someone else and feel good about ourselves. Such self-judgments can make us insecure and forget that it is through God's grace we are who we are. (I Corinthians 15:10, NLT) Grace does not judge. Grace does not look for faults in others. Grace does not condemn ourselves. Most of all, grace does not choose to live in guilt but rather in gratitude.

Many times we allow ourselves to live in the rat race of trying to be perfect and to look perfect to those around us. "For by one sacrifice he has made *perfect* forever those who are being made holy." (Hebrews 10:14, NIV) Sometimes, we can look at someone and believe that they are almost "perfect." They have "everything." But, in reality, we are *all* made perfect in him. We can live with joy and confidence in who we are because of Jesus.

One of my closest friends, Jennifer, used to live in the rat race of trying to look perfect in her life. Yet now, as a result of Christ's sacrifice in her life, she has redefined herself and is no longer afraid to show her true self. She has stopped living for outward perfection, but lives in the confidence of Christ. She presently lives in Cambodia as a missionary in conditions that are far less comfortable than what she grew up with in the United States. Yet, she does not complain or wish for a nicer life. She serves the church in Phnom Penh as well as the poor with joy and enthusiasm.

Jennifer did not start out her life in the normal way. She was an honor roll student, a beauty queen for the Philippines, and a Hoola champion. She went from beauty pageant to beauty pageant, winning many of them not only because of her beauty, but for her intelligence, talents and charisma. She had the world at her feet. She strove to attain perfection through her appearance, grades and activities. However, in all of this, she found nothing but emptiness and insecurity. She tried to fill the void with her boyfriend who was rich and handsome. In fact, he was one of the judges at one of her pageants. They fell in love, and she thought that she had found happiness, until she unexpectedly became pregnant.

When Jennifer found out that she was expecting a child, all that she had been living for came crashing down. There was no room for a baby in a beauty queen's life—at least not at that time. The choices were before her, and with pressure from her boyfriend, she agreed to an abortion. There are no words to express the horror and devastation she felt in having taken the life of her unborn baby. She was confused, empty and dejected. She felt her life spiral down into an endless abyss.

Soon afterward, she met a Christian who invited her to a Bible study group. She was astonished by God's word and his truths. She wanted the life that Jesus was calling her to. She called her boyfriend and told him that he, too, needed to read God's Word. As a result, he began to attend a Bible study as well. Within a short few weeks, both of them decided to make Jesus their Lord and Savior. And they were baptized into Christ.

Now Jennifer and Cesar are married and have three beautiful children. They have been serving in the ministry as missionaries in Asia for almost two decades. Their lives continue to impact hundreds and thousands as they pour out themselves to serve God. They are both an incredible example of people who give everything for God's kingdom just like their Lord and Savior did. I praise God for women like Jennifer. When she finally understood the grace of God, she chose to redefine her life, which was no longer defined by pageants, Hoola competitions and grades. She had become a daughter of God, defined by his grace.

Though we may not all be beauty queens, Friend, you are beautifully and wonderfully made—an amazing flower designed by God himself. He displays you with his grace. It is by grace that you have those academic or leadership abilities. It is by grace that you have a personality that exudes so much warmth that everyone wants to be around you. It is by grace that you are able to walk, to run and even compete in sports. It is by grace that you can speak in front of an audience and mesmerize them with your speeches. It is by grace that you have a job that you enjoy and look forward to. It is by grace that you are able to paint and draw amazing pictures that you can sell to others.

AND…it is by grace that you possess every weakness and frailty in your body, character and personality, because those very qualities helped you and even enabled you to accept God's wonderful grace.

AND…it is seeing God's grace at work in your imperfections that gives hope to those around you. So don't let the world define who you are. Let God's grace define the masterpiece of perfection that you are in his sight.

While I know that God's grace makes me perfect in his sight, I still need to fight against my sinful tendencies. As I mature in my appreciation of God's grace, I am more motivated to keep myself away from temptation and to pray more when I am tempted. I have learned to no longer focus on myself and on my feelings, but on God. Negative thoughts do not bombard my mind as much as they used to, and I can remain joyful through the difficulties.

So the next time you feel tempted to get down on yourself or to become insecure because of your weaknesses, look at yourself in the mirror and tell yourself, *"You are fearfully and wonderfully made. You are created exactly the way the Lord meant you to be. You have the grace of God in you so you don't have to be depressed about who you are. You are a beautiful flower in God's sight. God loves you."* Then, smile at yourself and continue to walk in gratitude for his grace.

 ## QUESTIONS FOR THE HEART

1. What is your perception of God's grace in your life right now? Do you feel like your definition is according to what you have heard over the years or from God's Word?

2. How has God used your weaknesses and shortcomings to guide you to him?

3. Write down the ways you have seen God's grace work in your life until now. Keep this list with you as you go through these pages.

Chapter 2

EVE: GOD'S GRACE TOWARD SIN

(Suggested reading: Genesis 2 and 3)
Try to imagine this scenario:

> A BMW and a show horse.
> A mansion and two summer homes.
> An unlimited bank account and shopping sprees at exclusives stores in
>   New York City.

Sound like a depiction of a modern Disney princess movie? Or perhaps the fruits of a successful financial career?

No, this was my life...at the age of sixteen. From the outside, anyone might have envied my life as a teenager. I had rich parents who could give me almost anything I wanted, including that unlimited bank account. My mother never questioned my purchases or told me that I could not buy something. My classmates were children of famous people, and I graduated from the same school as Jacqueline Kennedy Onassis. On weekends, my friends and I would go into New York City to eat at expensive restaurants, to watch Broadway shows, and of course, to shop at Tiffany's and sip tea at the Russian Tea Room. In every way, it could be said that I had a dream life.

Yet I lived with emptiness, doubts and regrets, not because I didn't have enough, but because all of these wonderful things did not keep me from my own sinful ways.

Consider Eve's life. She had everything a woman could have asked for. Paradise. Abundance. A perfect man. A nice figure. A life with all that anyone would want— this is the image I have of the Garden of Eden. Adam and Eve were given a great gift. They lived in the ultimate abode and had all that they needed to sustain a happy life. They were given power to rule over the fish in the sea, the birds of the air, and the creatures of the land. Yet sadly, all of this wondrous bounty and splendor in the Garden could not keep Adam and Eve from sinning. Simply put: a perfect world was not enough. They lived the dream life, but temptation lay in wait in the middle of the Garden.

Often, we want to believe that if we lived in a perfect world with no problems at work, home or school, we would be better people. We want to think that it is the trials and difficult people in our lives that cause us to sin. If it wasn't for those people or challenges, we would behave like "angels", wouldn't we? We would no longer get angry, irritated or exasperated. We would be wonderful and almost perfect people, right? But instead we have to deal with the critical in-law, the unreasonable teacher at school, the troublesome neighbor, the lazy and selfish husband, the oppressive dad or the unfair boss. Without them, life would be so easy, and we'd never sin…right?

Or perhaps you face challenging health issues—a child's disability or a handicap from an accident—or a failed business venture or the loss of a loved one. These difficulties can force us to battle with darkness in our hearts: bitterness, frustration, anger and envy. We may even be led into addictive sins, because we feel unable to cope with our problems.

Our trials and critics certainly challenge us, sometimes unbearably so. And yet, when we read the story of Eve, we face a sobering reality. Eve was a woman like us—and even in the midst of the "perfect" life, she chose to sin. Despite the absence of stress and strain, her perfect life was not enough to keep her from disobeying God.

Getting all that we want and wish for is not, and never will be, the solution to keeping us out of sin. No matter how many blessings we receive, we will not be prevented from having to face temptation. Even trying to create the "perfect world" for our own children won't keep them completely pure.

Unfortunately, no perfect world will keep us from messing up. For this reason God, in his wisdom, made provisions for us so that we could be forgiven despite our weaknesses and shortcomings. Those provisions were made because God knows how imperfect we are and tend to be.

Dealing with Temptation by Appreciating God's Grace

When tempted, no one should say, "God is tempting me." For God cannot be tempted by evil, nor does he tempt anyone; but each one is tempted when, by his own evil desire, he (she) is dragged away and enticed. Then, after desire has conceived, it gives birth to sin; and sin when it is full-grown, gives birth to death.

(James 1:13-15, NIV)

As we have already established, God is a loving God. But this fact should not make us feel empowered to sin whenever we want to. When God placed Adam in the Garden, there was no set of rules or laws that we know of. It seems that Adam was free to roam about and live as he pleased. The only prohibited act was eating the fruit from the tree of the knowledge of good and evil (Genesis 2:16-17), because it would cause them to die. Aside from that, God commanded Adam to work the garden and to take care of it.

The Bible is not clear about how long Adam and Eve were in the Garden before they disobeyed God nor does it explain why they decided to disregard him after being given all these wonderful blessings. Maybe they wanted some adventure in their perfect world, or they had simply become curious. Whatever the case may have been, in an expansive paradise, they were tempted by that one tree in the middle of the Garden. They could not get it out of their minds, leading them to go near the tree and to hang around it. Somehow, the Garden and its abundance were just not enough.

The story of Adam and Eve shows us how we would fare if given a chance to live in a world of plenty where everything was picture-perfect, and we would want for nothing. We would be just like Adam and Eve. It would only be a matter of time before we made the same mistake. They had no problems. God gave them life and was the perfect Father. He never abused them—no dysfunctional family or relatives to deal with. They never experienced or witnessed suffering, death or pain. They could not blame their pasts or their unresolved scars for their shortcomings, which are often reasons we use to rationalize our sinful behavior. This is not to negate how our backgrounds, experiences and upbringing do affect us, but the Bible makes it clear through the lives of Adam and Eve that even if men and women are given the optimal life, they can and will still mess up. Temptation eventually seizes us and makes us fall. A pristine garden, ideal circumstances, and a perfect father were not good enough to help these two human beings live without sin.

What can we learn from Adam and Eve? Unfortunately, we do not have the luxury of living in a perfect world. The sins of our world and the people around us influence and even pollute the way we think. Though we might not want to get high on drugs, friends can push us to "try it just once." Though we might not deliberately seek out porn, some websites are programmed to pop up hard-core ads when we least expect it. Though we didn't understand sex as children, men might have violated us at a young age. Those wounds, scars and memories do influence who we are and what we become. We are led to sin over and over again. Temptation surrounds us. It is not just one tree, but a forest of forbidden trees, their deadly fruit being eaten by everyone, almost every day. Much of the credit goes to Satan, because he is cunning and has succeeded in deceiving the world and in using our sinful natures against us.

Satan's Scheme in a Fallen World

So if Adam and Eve couldn't deal with temptation in a *perfect* world, how can we be expected to do so in this *fallen* world? We need to recognize Satan's tactics. Satan has a pattern in his strategy. Those tricks are revealed to us through the way he approached Adam and Eve. Though often seemingly complex, at the core, his methods have a common theme: They are all based on deception.

First of all, we can often fall into the deception of believing that somehow God has deprived us. *We deserve better.* Isn't that what the media and commercials say? Every day, we are bombarded by lies which slowly convince us that we do not have all that we "should."

As I write this, two men are running for our presidential elections. In many of the commercials, there is a common slogan: *You deserve a better president. You deserve a president who cares about your healthcare. You deserve a president who is concerned about your small business.* It is just a short jump from that message to an all-encompassing one:

You deserve a better life.

Satan is so good at weaving convincing lies.

The fact is that we really don't *deserve* anything good in this life. Anything good that we have is a *gift* from God. (James 1:16-18). God never tempts us or causes us to sin. (James 1:13). Instead, he gives us directions, encouragement and strength so that we will not fall.

God, in his graciousness, recognized that the serpent or Satan was the cause of Eve's downfall. God says that the serpent was "more crafty" than any other animal (Genesis 3:1). The scriptures also tell us that the serpent targets Eve first and successfully deceives her into eating the forbidden fruit.

> *For Adam was formed first, then Eve.* **And Adam was not the one deceived**; *it was the woman who was deceived and became a sinner.*
>
> (1 Timothy 2:14, NIV)

> *But I am afraid that just as* **Eve was deceived** *by the serpent's cunning, your minds may somehow be led astray from your sincere and pure devotion to Christ.*
>
> (2 Corinthians 11:3, NIV)

It was a very sad day when Eve allowed the cunning serpent to deceive her. She ended up believing his lies.

Secondly, Satan pulled Eve away from God by convincing her that there was something wrong with God and his Word. Satan's devious ways influenced Eve to believe terrible things about God—things that were not true at all. Satan's words were:

> *"You won't die!" the serpent replied to the woman. "God knows that your eyes will be opened as soon as you eat it, and you will be like God, knowing both good and evil."*
>
> *(Genesis 3:4-5, NLT)*

With subtlety, the serpent undermined God's commands—making them sound like he was less than the deeply loving Father they thought he was. It almost sounds like God was being tightfisted. Yet, how could she get anything more than what she already had? From our perspective, she was blessed beyond measure, and still, Satan was able to fool her and make her mistrust God's intentions for her.

Jesus told his disciples: *Keep watching and praying that you may not enter into temptation; the spirit is willing, but the flesh is weak.* (Matthew 26:41, NASB) He warned his disciples to watch and pray so that they would not give in to temptation. So much of prayer is calling out to God for help when we feel weak or uncertain.

A simple whisper to the Lord of lords from Adam and Eve would have been all it took for God to come to their rescue. They could have asked him face-to-face before making their tragic mistake. But instead of trusting God and drawing close to him, Eve drew away and relied on her own judgment, taking the first bite. Isn't this true of so many of us? We do not go to God, and we forget to pray when temptation hits us. Rather than allowing the Spirit to help us through the enticement, we draw away from the power of God that gives us strength to overcome and give in to our desires and the emotions of the moment.

Many times, Satan convinces us that there is something "good" in sin, and we have to do it or have it. In Eve's case, it was being like God and attaining knowledge. We need to remember that God gives us the tools to overcome. He says that he will always give us a way out when we are tempted (1 Corinthians 10:13). Many times, instead of taking the way out, we take the way in:

"Just this once…"

"I'll work on it later…"

"I know that I shouldn't, but…"

"Everyone else I know does it…"

In such ways, we rationalize our way into sin. Excuses and rationalizations fill our minds, as desire grows stronger and stronger. Who do you think puts those suggestions there?

Let us understand that temptation is not something we can "work on" like a talent, skill or a job. As performance-oriented beings, we might convince ourselves that we can somehow handle it or overcome if we stay strong. Though that may be true in one sense, temptation is an ever-present force in every person's life whether we are teens or great-grandmothers. No matter how hard we struggle or attempt to never sin, we will fail at one time or another. I don't want to discourage you, but this is the reality of how temptation works in everyone.

Thankfully, we can learn from the mistakes of our biblical forefathers who teach us through the scriptures how we can avoid the same sins and pitfalls. We can also consult wise and seasoned people in our churches any time we face challenges and temptations.

Irene was sixty years older than me and had been a Christian for over fifty years, during which time she had served as an overseas missionary and as an elder's wife. One time, I asked Irene whether she sometimes still sinned. She looked at me with surprise and said, "I sin every day, Erica. I will never be perfect until the day that I die, and Jesus takes me into his arms." I was stunned and asked her how she sinned, because to me, she seemed so godly! She gave me a list of sins, which, did not seem like "bad" sins at all. But, she decided each day that she would not let Satan deceive her into sinning. What encouraged me the most was that she was continuing to fight her sinful nature, staying faithful to God and never giving up. She also let me know that she made right choices in her life (not every time of course), but fought to build her faith consistently. Consequently, those decisions became a part of who she was—a godly and faithful woman who was full of grace.

Temptation is always there. Sin is crouching at our doorsteps. We will fall into the deception of Satan from time to time. But praise God that he had a plan through grace, an amazing plan available whenever we call upon him. He will draw near to us whenever we draw near to him. This grace should motivate us, move us and compel us to resist Satan's schemes.

> *He has saved us and called us to a holy life—not because of anything we have done but because of his own purpose and grace. This grace was given us in Christ Jesus before the beginning of time.*
>
> (2 Timothy 1:9, NIV)

I've Messed Up, Now What?

It was Christmas Day. Our house was lit with beautiful candles. We were busy preparing for our Christmas meal and not watching our girls closely. They were both playing when I noticed that some of the candles were out, and the smell of smoke permeated the room. Alarmed, I called out to the girls who were upstairs in their room, apparently hiding. As I walked up the stairs, I saw drippings of wax all the way up the wooden steps.

"Hey girls," I said. "What are you doing up there?"

"Oh nothing. Just playing," they answered from behind their bedroom door.

I entered their bedroom with my hands on my hips and asked, "What are you playing with? Did you play with the candles I told you not to touch?"

"Oh no. You told us not to touch those," they both chimed.

"Then, why are there candle drippings up the stairs leading to your room?"

"I don't know," piped up my oldest, while my younger daughter had a guilty expression etched on her face.

"Umm. I think that one of you or both of you were playing with the candles after I told you not to play with them."

Immediately, they started talking at once, blaming each other for touching the candles and bringing them up to the room. As I looked more closely inside their room, I saw a smoldering candle sending off a wisp of smoke, lying on its side on the floor of the bedroom, which frightened me. I ran to pick it up and said, "Girls, you could have caused a fire in our house!"

Needless to say, though we laugh about it now, our grown daughters never forgot that Christmas day. They call it the Christmas Day Massacre, a humorous exaggeration of the discipline that was later meted out by my husband. They had thought that since it was Christmas, we would not punish them for what they had done. However, they had not only disobeyed us, but they had also lied to us. In the same way, God gives us an admonition:

> *My child, do not reject the Lord's discipline, and don't get angry when he corrects you. The Lord corrects those he loves, just as parents correct the child they delight in.*
>
> (Proverbs 15:5, NCV)

When Eve sinned, she did not want to face her sin right away, but blamed the serpent. Her statement was technically true, and God heard her reasoning, but ultimately Eve did not take responsibility for her sin. I listened to my daughters explain how they had brought the candles up into their room and played with them. They blamed each other for what had happened. Neither of them took full responsibility for playing with fire and lying about it. But they knew that they had blown it, so they were hiding in their room. It was not fun disciplining them for their disobedience and deceit, especially since it was Christmas day. They learned a lesson, however, that they still remember to this day as grown women.

Excuses and rationalization are a part of human nature. We can *always* cite a reason why we sinned. It might be best friends who said extremely hurtful things that we can't let go of. It could be a husband who continues to do the same thing over and over, never changing and always causing frustration. Maybe teachers give bad grades, because they don't "like" us. These "reasons" create in us the justification to get angry, be unforgiving, and retaliate with hurtful actions and words. All the while, we are convinced that what we did is not as bad as what someone else did.

Adam and Eve covered themselves with fig leaves and hid in the trees. God knew where they were even as they hid. God knew what they had done, but shame and fear drew them away from him. Their own guilt made them want to "cover up" to look good on the outside with the hope that no one would notice, especially God, their Father.

Some of us don't even try to hide. We have rationalized our sin to the point where we don't feel the guilt or consequences anymore. We have hardened our hearts and avoid facing the reality of what we have done. Inevitably, we blame others or the situation. Nothing is completely our fault. It is the way we escape and try to evade the ramifications of our actions. But this leaves a trail of devastation for the people closest to us.

We all have a choice. We can either hate the correction and discipline, or we can embrace the truth and be set free. Ultimately, Adam and Eve chose to admit their sin. They both confessed to what they had done against God. Accordingly, Adam and Eve had to face God's discipline and the consequence of their sin.

> *To the woman he said, "I will greatly increase your pains in childbearing; with pain you will give birth to children. Your desire will be for your husband, and he will rule over you."*
>
> (Genesis 3:16, NIV)

My friend Reba was fifteen years old when she became pregnant. She had never imagined that the "one time" would alter her life. She felt panic after she missed her period the first month. She thought it would come sooner or later. Before she knew it, three months had gone by, and she was wrought with morning sickness every day. When she told her boyfriend about her pregnancy, he was horrified. He said that he was too young to be a dad, so he broke up with her and left Reba to make an important decision all alone.

This is a common story among many women today. It was that one night or the few times with no consequences that made them do it again…and again. The forbidden fruit looked good and even tasted delicious at the time. It was afterward that left both Adam and Eve naked and guilty. Their eyes had been opened, but only after it was too late. They sewed fig leaves together and hid from God.

In the same way, when the pregnancy test came out positive for Reba, there was a temptation to hide, to run away and to somehow "fix it". According to US statistics, nearly half (46%) of teenagers 15-19 years old have had sex at least one time. Thirteen percent of teens 15 and under have had intercourse. By the time they are 19 years old, seven out of ten have engaged in sexual activity. Each year an average of 750,000 teen girls between the ages of 15 and 19 become pregnant. About 30% of these pregnancies end in abortion, and about 15% end in miscarriages, while the rest give birth. But most of these births involve girls who are 18-19 years old.

With such statistics, what did Reba do? At the young age of fifteen, Reba chose life. She gave birth to a beautiful baby girl and decided to raise her with the help of her parents while continuing through high school. When she turned eighteen, she moved out on her own with her daughter, Tonya. Unfortunately, she did not change her lifestyle and continued to have relationships with other men. But when Tonya turned nine, God came into Reba's life. A Christian reached out to her and helped her to see God's grace, and she made the decision to become a Christian. Her life was completely transformed. She repented of her immoral ways and became a new creation through Christ.

Reba made the wrong choices at first, but learned from them. She decided to keep Tonya when she had the option to end the pregnancy. Her one wrong decision taught her to make the right decision. When it mattered most, she chose life and has never regretted her choice. Almost a decade later, she made another crucial decision, which was to choose Jesus Christ and make him Lord of her life. Her conversion impacted her daughter who has never made the same mistakes as her mother.

Today, Reba is happily married to a Christian man, and her daughter is also married to a wonderful Christian man. When Tonya wore white at her wedding, it reflected the purity of her life and her relationship with her fiancé. Reba's spiritual decision had given her daughter a chance to live differently. Because Reba faced her sin, she was able to truly experience the grace of God and to give it to others.

God's grace is amazing. He gives us second chances even after we have made mistakes. This is true not just with teenage pregnancy but with every sin in our lives whether it is cheating, lying, stealing, anger or gossip. I share Reba's story as an illustration to show the extent of God's grace in our lives.

All of us will make mistakes and sin. We will even suffer consequences, but these repercussions can help us to make the right choices the second time around. Seeing our failings teaches us to grow, which, in turn, helps us to mature and increase our faith. When we refuse to look at how we have wronged someone or committed a sin, we miss out on truly understanding the grace of God.

We can sometimes imagine thunderbolts coming down from heaven to zap us after we have blown it. We often believe that something really bad will happen, because God is mad at us. And even if nothing comes showering down on us, we inflict punishment on ourselves, pouring on the guilt and shame. We seem to create our own form of thunderbolts and lightning, hating ourselves and hiding from others so that they will never see our "true" selves. We can even hide ourselves from those closest to us: our spouses, our siblings and our parents.

God is patient. He does not want to zap us with thunderbolts. He is willing to wait in the hope that we will change. Even though God is willing, let us decide to not make God wait too long. *The Lord is not slow in keeping his promise, as some understand slowness. He is patient with you, not wanting anyone to perish, but everyone to come to repentance.* (2 Peter 3:9, NIV)

How did our infamous Christmas Day Massacre end up? It was one of our family's most memorable Christmases, because we were able to talk about God's greatest gift in Christ—his grace. After some discipline, we, of course, forgave our girls for their disobedience. The girls did not remain depressed through the rest of the day, but they were happy for the rest of the night. There was no lingering distance, but instead much love, closeness, and presents! In the same way, we can take hold of God's grace by accepting who we are before his throne. When we accept our true selves, we can truly appreciate God's bountiful, intimate, and blessed grace.

God's Perfect Grace to Each of Us

It was early evening, December 4, 1981. I sat in the back pew of the church, wanting with all my heart to make Jesus Lord of my life, but struggling with the notion that I had too many sins for God to forgive. I thought that it would not matter how many times I asked for forgiveness or how much water was used at my baptism; my sins were far too many for God to ever wash away. I had been sobbing about this for half an hour while sitting in the back pew of the church sanctuary. A kind young man, who had been a Christian for several years, sat down next to me.

He asked me, "Why are you crying?"

"I know I have sinned too much for God to ever forgive me," I replied.

He sat next to me, patiently listening to my dilemma. When I was done, he said to me gently, "Everyone has tons of sins, far more than we could ever count. Do you believe that God created the heavens and the earth in six days then rested on the seventh?"

"Yes," I replied.

"Do you believe that Jesus was sent on this earth for us?"

"Yes," I said again.

"Do you believe that Jesus was crucified for our sins?"

"Yes," I answered. By this time, I was wondering what all this had to do with my problem.

Finally, he asked, "Do you believe that Jesus was raised from the dead on the third day."

"Yes, yes." I said impatiently.

Then he looked at me with the most loving expression and asked, "Then why can't you believe that this powerful, wonderful and amazing God, who created the heavens and the earth, who sent his son to die for our sins and who raised him up on the third day, can forgive all your sins?"

My eyes clouded with tears. I had believed all these impossible things about God, but could not believe that he could forgive one person's sins: mine.

Forgiveness is a concept that is very hard for some of us to accept. We look at ourselves and cannot fathom how we can be forgiven after all that we have done. Forgiving ourselves can be difficult, much less accepting forgiveness from a perfect God. We feel like we deserve punishment, not mercy. We can beat ourselves up for years after we have sinned, feeling ashamed and humiliated.

After their fall, Adam and Eve were definitely punished for their disobedience. Yes, they had to leave the Garden. Yes, Adam had to work the soil. Yes, Eve had to bear children in pain and suffering. Yet, before God carried out his decree, he covered their shame. Adam and Eve no longer had to use fig leaves, a shabby and flimsy form of covering, but God gave them better clothing. In order for that to happen, God made his first sacrifice. He took the lives of two animals to create these new coverings for Adam and Eve. (Genesis 3:21) It was after this act of kindness—grace—that he sent them from the Garden of Eden, away from paradise. God, in his infinite mercy and compassion, did not destroy Adam and Eve, but covered their disgrace and continued to love them despite their betrayal.

He had given them a perfect world to live in. He had blessed them with many talents. He had given them the chance to live with him in paradise. But even in a perfect world, man and woman still needed grace. If God showed grace to two people in a perfect world, how much more will he shower his grace on us, who live in an imperfect and fallen world? His grace is perfect. It was perfect in paradise, and it has not changed. Moreover, his grace is perfect in our imperfect world today.

Before becoming a Christian, I reasoned that I had to become "perfect" first in order to be forgiven. If I was not "cleaned up" enough, I thought that God would not allow me into his kingdom. In my foolishness, I was striving to be good enough to deserve forgiveness. In my struggle to achieve this perfection, I felt like a failure and decided to stop going to church. During what I had decided would be my last visit to church, that kind man saw through my tears and helped me to understand that my comprehension of God and his grace was misconstrued.

After they sinned, Adam and Eve hid themselves in the trees. They did not try to change or to "fix" their mistake. They did not profusely apologize for their transgression. They did not kneel before God begging for mercy. They did nothing to merit God's forgiveness, and their repentance was far from perfect. Even though God knew what they had done, he still asked them if they had eaten from the forbidden tree. They answered truthfully, confessing their disobedience.

Unlike Adam and Eve, we do not live in paradise. Our world is filled with flaws and temptations. Every day we are surrounded by daily enticements. We can try to live a pure life and strive to be righteous in every way, but the deception of this world pulls us away time and time again even as we try to strive to be like Christ. Sometimes we can become hardened to the sin around us and tolerate immoral behavior, not out of evil intent, but out of spiritual dullness.

As his children, we must learn to recognize the difference between good and evil by staying in his Word. He didn't create us to be robots without a free will, so it is up to us to use our ability to choose and to do what is right. This freedom allows us to sin or to be righteous. At the same time, God also understands that we are weak beings with a sinful nature and capable of falling even after trying our best.

After Adam and Eve received their punishment, they did not become sinless. Though they had a perfect Father as an example, they did not become picture-perfect parents either. We all know what happened to Cain and Abel, their children. (Read Genesis 4:1-16) Both Cain and Abel sacrificed to God, but only Abel's sacrifice was accepted. This caused jealousy in Cain who ended up killing his brother, Abel. In the same way, no matter how hard we try; we will always make mistakes in our lives. Only God's grace is flawless. His impeccable grace is the only hope for us in this defective and lacking world. The sacrifice he made is what can clothe us with perfection:

> *For by one sacrifice he has made perfect forever those who are being made holy.*
>
> (Hebrews 10:14, NIV)

This is the wonderful hope that we have in Christ. We can be made perfect, not through who we are or how hard we try, but through the sacrifice of our Lord. God is the only one who can make us holy and perfect in his sight. Perfection is found only in his grace.

After their sin, Adam and Eve lived in an imperfect world. To this day, we reap the consequences of Adam and Eve's disobedience. We live in a flawed society with people who sin against one another every day. From the beginning, God saw that no matter how perfect a life we humans were given, at some point we would mess up, because we are weak in our flesh. Adam and Eve came into the world first, and they were the first ones to sin. If we had been placed in paradise with the same choices, it is almost certain that it would have only been a matter of time before we too fell into sin.

The vicious cycle of sin has continued from one generation to another, and finally reaches down to us. God knows the transgressions, weaknesses and shortcomings that lie in each one of us. He has shown us so much grace despite these failings. If we could just see the continued blessings of his grace through the hard times and the challenges in our lives, we would be grateful people ready to give our very best to God all the time. And instead of wasting days and even years blaming others and circumstances we cannot control, we can find hope through admitting our faults and taking responsibility for our sins, because we know God's grace is there for us.

Those of us who incessantly destroy our own self-esteem over our sins can learn to accept God's perfect grace so that we will be able to live differently. This will also teach us to extend grace to those around us. Hopefully, in all of this, we will be motivated to give our all instead of being immobilized by our guilt and shame.

> *Here it is in a nutshell: Just as one person did it wrong and got us in all this trouble with sin and death, another person did it right and got us out of it. But more than just getting us out of trouble, he got us into life! One man said no to God and put many people in the wrong; one man said yes to God and put many in the right.*
>
> *All that passing laws against sin did was produce more lawbreakers. But sin didn't, and doesn't, have a chance in competition with the aggressive forgiveness we call grace. When it's sin versus grace, grace wins hands down. All sin can do is threaten us with death, and that's the end of it. Grace, because God is putting everything together again through the Messiah, invites us into life—a life that goes on and on and on, world without end.*
>
> (Romans 5:18-21, The Message)

The world might have viewed my wealthy, extravagant life as a perfect life—but it was not perfect at all. All my family's money had only brought sorrow upon sorrow, mistrust upon suspicion among family and friends, as well as infidelity upon betrayal. Bit by bit, riches and wealth contributed to eroding and destroying the bonds in my family. Thankfully, over the years, God has re-educated me about how to build a healthy and loving family, and through the guidance of wise and spiritual men and women, I have discovered what was missing from my so-called "perfect" life as a teenager: the reassurance and the motivation of God's perfect grace.

Now, after many years in Christ, although I strive to be my best for God, like my friend Irene, I am far from living a perfectly righteous life. My sins as a Christian have and continue to hurt people around me. Ironically, I have probably hurt most, the people I love the most: my husband and my children. I still need God's grace.

There is a vicious cycle that will continue in our bloodlines, if each of us does not decide to faithfully live by the grace of God and let go of the scars left over from our past experiences. I know that I have had to decide to break many sinful patterns through the Spirit of God inside of me. I have had to learn to say "no" to my sinful nature. Of course, I still fail even as I try with all my effort to be different. In some areas, I am sometimes still like Eve and try to hide, finding flimsy "fig leaves" like blaming others to cover up my guilt. In other ways, however, the Spirit has helped me to completely repent and become a new creation in Christ. This has never been on my own strength, but always through the power of his grace.

Will I ever deserve his grace? Will I ever be perfect enough to earn his grace? No. But the blood of Christ cleanses me every day, making me perfect before my God and giving me a new start and a new hope. Let us all rejoice in God's perfect grace as we live in this imperfect world as imperfect beings. His grace has no limits!

 ## QUESTIONS FOR THE HEART

1. Take time out to read Genesis 3:1-13. What was Eve's attitude towards temptation? How do you deal with temptation in your life compared to Eve?

2. When you look at your life, you may see many problems. Now, imagine everything being perfect. Be honest with yourself. What sins would you struggle with in your life. What are one or two weaknesses you see in your sinful nature?

3. Ask God today for forgiveness in areas that you haven fallen short and make a decision to be different from Eve the next time the temptation comes your way.

Chapter 3

SARAH: GRACE THROUGH FAITH

The Princess of the Multitude
(Suggested reading: Genesis 12-14)

If we met Sarah at a tea party, many of us might struggle with envy because of her beauty, wealth and happy marriage. She was so beautiful that both a Pharaoh of Egypt and the King of Gerar wanted to take her to be their wife (Genesis 12:14-16, Genesis 20:1-2). She was wealthy enough that when her husband, Abraham, was offered the plunder of Sodom after helping to conquer four kings, he refused (Genesis14: 21-22). She was loved enough that when she was angry and frustrated with her slave, Hagar, Abraham told her to do what she wanted to her maidservant (Genesis 16:6). Abraham had no emotional attachment to Hagar, even though she was the mother of his first-born. His priority was to Sarah and to her alone until her death.

In Hebrew, Sarai (the original spelling for Sarah) means *my princess.* Sar means *prince,* and its feminine form is Sara. The *i* adds the possessive form to mean *my.* When it finally came time for Sarai to bear a son, God changed her name to Sarah *(princess of the multitude)*. Looking at Sarah's life, we can see that she, in many ways, was truly like a princess. She was beautiful. She was intelligent. She traveled extensively. She was married to a wealthy man who was considered to be a prince by the Hittites (Genesis 23:6) She also had a maidservant that did her bidding. On top of all of this, her husband loved her very much.

Princess of Grace

From the very beginning, God's plan for Sarah's life was for her to be the princess of the multitude, the mother of faith—the mother of all who would live by faith. She was meant not only to bear those children from her own body, but also to represent the start of the new covenant based on faith and not on the law. She is the spiritual mother of all of us who are heirs of God's promise (Galatians 3:29).

According to Paul's letter to the Galatians, Sarah represents God's grace as the free woman, not under the law of the first covenant but under grace through the covenant of faith.

> *For it is written that Abraham had two sons, one by the slave woman and the other by the free woman. His son by the slave woman was born in the ordinary way; but his son by the free woman was born as the result of a promise. These things may be taken figuratively, for the women represent two covenants. One covenant is from Mount Sinai and bears children who are to be slaves: This is Hagar. Now Hagar stands for Mount Sinai in Arabia and corresponds to the present city of Jerusalem, because she is in slavery with her children. But the Jerusalem that is above is free, and she is our mother.*
>
> (Galatians 4:22-26, NIV)

In other words, we are all born of the free woman Sarah, if we live by faith and are redeemed through faith. But those who live under the law continue to be slaves of the old covenant and therefore are the children of Hagar. Legalism and the law can re-enslave us. If we are not careful, our Christianity can become a set of "do's" and "don'ts." We then end up living under guilt and constant self-condemnation rather than with gratitude and love for God. Even if we believe in God's love, we can fall into legalism if we consider his love something to be earned rather than accepted.

> *It is for freedom that Christ set us free. Stand firm, then, and do not let yourselves be burdened again by the yoke of slavery... You who are trying to be justified by law have been alienated from Christ; you have fallen away from grace.*
>
> (Galatians 5:1, 4, NIV)

When we allow ourselves to live by the law, we alienate ourselves from Christ and fall away from grace. At the same time, it can be hard to balance faith in God's grace with a life of holiness. On one hand, we can create rule upon rule for ourselves in order to "measure up" to a certain level of spirituality. On the other hand, we can get lax about our need to remain pure before God and rationalize serious sins in our lives that should be confessed and repented of.

One thing is for sure: we can never be perfect enough. No matter how much we fight against it, we will sin again and again. Therefore, Paul reminds us to be careful not to burden ourselves with the chains of unnecessary requirements—i.e., legalism—and fall away from grace. At the same time, Paul also encourages us in that chapter about how we were called to be free, but that we shouldn't use our freedom to indulge in the sinful nature (Galatians 5:13)

We have a choice: we can choose to not to live in sin any longer. We need to remember and to believe that we are children of Sarah, the princess of the multitude. If we are her children, then we, too, are princesses— "spiritual" princesses in Christ. Peter tells us that we are her daughters if we do what is right and do not give way to fear (1 Peter 3:6). It is fear that often makes us sin— whether worry, anger, frustration or lying. We must not give in to fear when we are tempted.

I have three daughters, and it is quite amusing how each of them identifies with a different Disney princess. My second daughter, Manami, loves Ariel and Rapunzel. She relates with Ariel, because Ariel was a performer and dreamed of a world beyond her natural borders. And she relates to Rapunzel who wanted to do the "right" thing, but was also enamored by the outside world, which was forbidden to her. At the same time, both Ariel and Rapunzel deeply wanted to please their parents, King Triton (Ariel's father) and Gothel (Rapunzel's mother).

When Manami was a little girl and even until recently, she always wanted to especially please her father. She desired his approval so much that she would do anything to make him proud. Being raised in Japan taught her that doing all the "right" things and following all the rules would gain that acceptance and approval. What she didn't realize was that no matter what she did, her father was always proud of her and loved her unconditionally.

There is an innate longing in us women to seek approval and to want to be valued for who we are. We want to be princesses to the men in our lives. We want to be valued and precious to them. We want to be extra special in their lives. This desire translates into our relationship with God. We want approval from our Lord, which is good. But sometimes we try so hard that we can wear ourselves out.

The apostle Peter indicates that we have been given a special role as God's elect.

> But you are a chosen race, a royal priesthood, a dedicated nation, [God's] own purchased, special people, that you may set forth the wonderful deeds and display the virtues and perfections of Him who called you out of darkness into His marvelous light.
>
> (1 Peter 2:9 AMP)

We are not called by God to be enslaved by the rules and regulations that some of us place on ourselves. Instead, God intended for us to be his special daughters, royal princesses, treasured and cherished by him and unencumbered by the weight of sin. Understanding the fact that we are chosen and purchased to display the virtues and perfections of God should trigger a deep desire in us to escape the cravings of this world and live to solely please our Father in heaven.

Princess of Blessing
(Suggested Reading: Genesis 21-23)

Sarah is not just the princess of the multitude, because she represents the new covenant. Through God's grace, she gave birth to Isaac (Genesis 21:1). She bore the child that became the heir of the promise—the seed that would spread, making Abraham's descendants like the stars in the sky and the sand on the seashore (Genesis 22:17). The child came as a result of God's promise, not because of Sarah's righteousness or pure life. In fact, right after Isaac was weaned, Sarah wanted Abraham to get rid of Hagar and her son. This request distressed Abraham (Genesis 21:11). As a result of Sarah's heartless request, Hagar and her son almost died in the desert from a lack of food and water. Even a princess has her ugly pettiness and weaknesses!

When I look at my life, I see how so many times God blessed me despite myself. I have character flaws that may never change, which God tolerates through his grace. He even forgives the way my failings hurt those I love, even though I may not be aware that I have messed up. I once had a dream that God took me into heaven and showed me its beauty. But in the center, there was a room that had files of all my sins. If I wanted to, I could go inside that room for a few minutes to see how I had been forgiven. Well, being a curious person, I entered the room. Within seconds, I heard recordings of my voice on days when I was frustrated and angry at my children. I could not stand being there for even a few seconds, so I ran out. God told me in my dream that he had forgiven me for all of those sins. When I woke up, I apologized to my girls for acting poorly when I was in a bad mood!

Sarah lived to be a hundred and twenty-seven years old. She lived to see her son become an adult. She was neither a perfect wife nor a perfect mother. All the same, Abraham loved her deeply. When she passed away, her husband wept over her and bought her a tomb fit for a princess.

Then Abraham rose from beside his dead wife and spoke to the Hittites. He said, "I am an alien and a stranger among you. Sell me some property for a burial site here so I can bury my dead." The Hittites replied to Abraham, "Sir, listen to us. You are a mighty prince among us. Bury your dead in the choicest of our tombs. None of us will refuse you his tomb for burying your dead."

(Genesis 23:3-6, NIV)

Even in death, Sarah was considered a princess. Because the Hittites viewed Abraham as a prince, they offered to give him the choicest of all burial sites for free. Abraham, however, insisted on paying the full price of the land and purchased a gravesite fit for royalty. It was deeded to him, and he was able to bury Sarah, *his* princess (*Sarai*) at the finest location of their time.

None of us has to be perfect to be used by God. He will use us despite ourselves. God's promises do not depend on our actions. Even though we're imperfect, God can find a way to make his promises come true. *For if the inheritance depends on the law, then it no longer depends on a **promise;** but God in his grace gave it to Abraham through a **promise.*** (Galatians 3:18, NIV) *If you belong to Christ, then you are Abraham's seed, and heirs according to the **promise.*** (Galatians 3:29, NIV)

In this way, God's grace should keep us humble. There is nothing that we personally do that makes God's promises come to fruition. It is up to God to execute his plans and to carry out his will. When we look back at the end of our lives, we probably will be shocked at how many promises he has fulfilled in our lives despite our sins, mistakes and bad judgment calls. That is how God's grace worked in Sarah's life, and so it will with us. Praise the Lord.

Wait on the Lord
(Suggested Reading: Genesis 16)

For I know the plans I have for you," declares the Lord, "plans to prosper you and not to harm you, plans to give you hope and a future. Then you will call upon me and come and pray to me, and I will listen to you.

(Jeremiah 29:11-12, NIV)

God has a plan for each of our lives. It is a great plan, full of promise. Yet, as women, we can get impatient with God's plans. We have our own plans that we want to put into action right away. We like to run ahead and make our desires become reality. Many of us do not like God's timing in certain areas of our lives. This can include meeting the man of our dreams, when to have children, or when we get to buy that one special item. Sometimes, waiting for these things can feel beyond what we can handle.

God had a plan for Sarah, but she ran ahead of God and tried to take control when she did not get pregnant right away. She made her husband sleep with her maidservant, Hagar, rather than trusting in God. She became impatient when God wanted her to wait. She was married to the man known as the father of faith. Yet, when we look at both of their lives, it becomes apparent that they needed to grow in their faith at key points.

None of us begins with amazing faith. Look closely at Abraham's life. He gave away his wife twice out of fear. In my opinion, giving in to fear is the exact opposite of faith. What is admirable on Sarah's part is that she was willing to submit to her husband—to go along with Abram's (as he was known then) crazy plan to protect his life. He even lied and told Pharaoh that Sarah was his sister! Okay, technically, she was actually his half-sister, so it may not have been a total lie in Abram's mind—if there is such an excuse.

Sarah faced so many different challenges to her faith and trust in God. From taking care of Abraham's nephew Lot, to moving from place to place, and then finally to being given away to two different men because of her beauty. Many of us might have felt like kicking our husbands out of the house for making us take care of his relatives for extended amounts of time. Others of us might have gotten frustrated at them for dragging us from city to city and never allowing us to settle in one place. Some of us would have shouted, "Divorce!" if our husband had given us away to strangers to save their own lives, not to mention doing it twice!

In many ways, Sarah was an admirable woman who was able to withstand circumstances that might have crushed other women. She resisted the temptation to take matters into her own hands...until it came to her inability to bear offspring. Nothing brought more anguish and stress on Sarah than her unfulfilled desire for a baby. She waited and waited, but the child never came. Abraham told her that God had promised them children. But she became impatient and began to doubt: *Maybe it's not supposed to be through us but just through Abraham. Maybe I'm keeping my husband from fulfilling God's promise, so I should do something about it. Maybe I need to find another woman who can bear my children, so that God's promises can be fulfilled. Yes, that's it! My husband gave me to those other men. So I can let him have another woman.*

Whatever was going through Sarah's mind, it probably came down to how to solve God's "slowness" in keeping his promise. Sarah's biological clock was running out, and perhaps her internal alarm was ringing after pushing the snooze button too many times. In her mind, waiting had become unbearable. As old age approached, holding tight until God would grant her a child no longer seemed like an option. But trusting and waiting for God's timing is a part of God's plan for each of our lives.

So many of the psalmists express yearnings and desires as they waited on the Lord.

> *I **wait** for the **LORD**, my soul waits, and in his word I put my hope. My soul waits for the **Lord** more than watchmen **wait** for the morning, more than watchmen **wait** for the morning.*
>
> (Psalm 130:5-6, NIV)

There is not a woman in the world who doesn't have unfulfilled desires. We have all wanted something, but some dreams may not be within our grasps. Our unrequited desires may have been to become Broadway stars, gold medal Olympians, or to marry the prince of some faraway country. On the other hand, it might not be such a far-fetched desire, but rather something that "everyone else has," like a husband, a child, a great job or a healthy body. And no matter how long we wait, those dreams may not come to fruition for some of us.

But we can have hope. God may have a very different plan for us. He gently tells us: ***Wait** for the LORD; be strong and take heart and **wait** for the LORD.* (Psalm 27:14, NIV) His plan may not be what we had imagined for ourselves. But believe it or not, it is a better plan and created specifically for us.

Marlene Heese is a dear friend. She has inspired my faith in so many ways by her devotion to God. She has also been an example of a woman who has waited on the Lord for many things in her life. The main area for her was being patient about having a child.

From the time that Marlene married Jim, they had wanted a child. Several years later, after having spent tens of thousands of dollars on surgeries to treat her endometriosis and several fertilization treatments, they were still not able to have children. In the end, the doctors informed her that it would not be possible for her to give birth to a child. It was heartbreaking for her, but she decided to hold on to the scripture in Psalm 113:9: "He settles the childless woman in her home as a happy mother of children."

After six years of marriage, they began to pray for a child to adopt. They were going to adopt a boy from Arizona. At the last minute it did not work out and sadness filled their hearts again. Then an opportunity came for them to adopt twin boys from the state of North Carolina. They were so excited and began making arrangements. This also fell through at the last moment. By this time, Marlene's heart was broken, and she felt as though her dreams had been crushed again and again. She begged God for a child, but seemingly he kept saying, "No."

Finally, they pursued adopting a child from China. In August 1999, they flew to China and picked up their little two-and-half-year-old daughter named Fuqin. They renamed her Alexandria. She was born in May of 1997, which was the exact month they had started praying to adopt a child. When the woman from the adoption center placed Alexandria in Marlene's arms, the little girl said, "Mama," and kissed her. Marlene melted, because God had finally allowed her to be a mother. It was not how she had planned it, but it was certainly how God had planned it to be. They immediately wanted another child and returned a few years later to adopt their second daughter Christina, who is such a delight and total joy to them.

Alexandria's adoption date was August 7, 1999. Exactly twelve years later on August 7, 2011, she made a decision to become a Christian. Her Father in heaven eternally adopted her on the same date just twelve years later! After years of waiting, there was so much joy and celebration. The Heeses are such a close family—much closer and connected than many other families I know. I really respect their faith and their perseverance so much.

Yet, Marlene and Jim did not stop there. Because they had adopted two Chinese girls, their heartfelt desire was to learn Chinese and to visit China. Recently, Jim's career took them to China, and then to Thailand where their family is very active in the church. By their faith, this couple is similar to Abraham and Sarah fighting as they help the people of Asia.

Here's the most unbelievable fact. If God had wanted to give Sarah a dozen children, he could have done so. Sarah could have ended up with two or three or ten sons rather than just one. Instead, God chose to give her Isaac and only Isaac. Why would God allow her to go through so many years of waiting? Why didn't he just give her a son right away to give his descendants a head start?

We have all been through the route that Sarah took—taking matters into our own hands rather than waiting on the Lord. What could God possibly want from us to make us wait on him? Why does he allow us to go through such agony? Well, when we look at both Abraham and Sarah's lives, we see the result. They are the father and mother of our faith. Waiting on the Lord helps us to become men and women of faith.

God eventually granted Abraham and Sarah a son, but even that was not without its challenges. When Isaac was still a young toddler, God asked Abraham to sacrifice his son. How do you think Sarah felt when her husband took Isaac up the mountain to sacrifice him? The Bible doesn't mention an argument or fight between Sarah and Abraham during this heart-rending time. I have a feeling that God would have recorded it if they had, because many of the faults of the Bible's great spiritual heroes are listed in its pages.

After all that waiting, it looked as though God was going to take that special child away. But when Abraham drew his knife to slay his son, God stopped him just seconds before the blade struck the boy. Then, God provided a ram to sacrifice in his place. God kept stretching and stretching Abraham and Sarah's faith until it was perfectly molded for his purposes. Ultimately, it is written in Romans that their faith was credited to them as righteousness.

Here's a question: Did Abraham and Sarah have incredible faith throughout their lives? Absolutely not. In fact, Abraham repeatedly gave in to fear and lied. Sarah gave in to fear and became controlling and manipulative.

However, when God talks about them in the Bible, it is with complete grace.

Yet he did not waver through unbelief regarding the promise of God,
but was strengthened in his faith and gave glory to God, being fully

persuaded that God had power to do what he had promised. This is why "it was credited to him as righteousness." The words "it was credited to him" were written not for him alone, but also for us, to whom God will credit righteousness—for us who believe in him who raised Jesus our Lord from the dead.

(Romans 4:20-24, NIV)

God does not expect perfection. This is where his grace is amazing. Despite all their weaknesses and shortcomings, God still lifts up Abraham and Sarah as those with amazing faith. The faith that they had was sufficient enough for God to work through. They may have struggled with how he was going to do it, but ultimately, they believed in his promise.

In the same way, each of us will struggle through our faith as we wait on God. His plans may not fit exactly with our plans. At times, we may feel like he has the exact opposite plan than ours. We will go through times of doubt, confusion, and fear. But let's allow God to stretch our faith, believing in his promise, so that he can fulfill his perfect plan for our lives through his grace.

Righteousness through Imperfect Faith
(Suggested Reading: Genesis 18)

As we saw earlier, Sarah did not have perfect faith. In fact, when two angels visited Abraham and Sarah with the good news of her having a child, Sarah laughed—and it wasn't because she believed. Imagine laughing at God because you don't think he can deliver.

One of them said, "I'm coming back about this time next year. When I arrive, your wife Sarah will have a son." Sarah was listening at the tent opening, just behind the man. Abraham and Sarah were old by this time, very old. Sarah was far past the age for having babies. Sarah laughed within herself, "An old woman like me? Get pregnant? With this old man of a husband?" God said to Abraham, "Why did Sarah laugh saying, 'Me? Have a baby? An old woman like me?' Is anything too hard for God? I'll be back about this time next year and Sarah will

have a baby." Sarah lied. She said, "I didn't laugh," because she was
afraid. But he said, "Yes you did; you laughed."

(Genesis 18:10-15, The Message)

It was a tough day. On top of doubting, Sarah lied when God confronted her about her laughing! God told her that there was nothing too hard for him to do and repeated that she would have a baby the following year. Then Sarah looked at Abraham and thought, *With this old man of a husband?* (Don't you love how the Bible keeps it real?)

Yet, we know the rest of the story. When Isaac was born, Sarah said, "God has brought me laughter and everyone who hears about this will laugh with me." (Genesis 21:6) No one who reads about Sarah in this passage can just pass over it without being amazed. Many of us smile and laugh because of the joy that shines through this story.

Scientifically, of course, it is physically impossible for a ninety-year-old woman to give birth. According to an article posted on Mail on Line and later aired on 20/20,[1] a sixty-nine-year-old woman gave birth to a daughter—the oldest recorded birth in modern times. But this was only possible through in-vitro fertilization. Sarah, of course, did not have the luxury of such advanced medical technology.

No matter how you look at it, any birth is a miracle. For any parent to witness their child's birth is a marvelous experience, especially for the mother who is actually giving birth. There is always much laughter and celebration, with families opening bottles of champagne, passing out cigars or sending out mass emails and texts. Of course, the current generation immediately posts volumes of photos on Facebook or Instagram. First-time parents feel like they have seen the greatest miracle of their lives. Second, third and fourth-time, most parents never cease to be astounded by the miracle and joy of a life coming into the world. It is truly a time of great happiness and marks an important event.

When we had our first child, my husband Frank went out to eat at a restaurant near the hospital and spontaneously announced to the whole restaurant that he had just had his first child. He felt no embarrassment in standing up and telling the whole world, because he was simply thrilled.

All the customers in the restaurant gave him a standing ovation! The owner of the restaurant kindly shared his joy and gave my husband a free glass of champagne. A few years later, Frank tried to visit the spot where the restaurant should have been, but it was not there. There was no trace of it. It was like the musical "Brigadoon", or some movie where a place appears for one special moment. Could angels have created that restaurant for that one brief moment, just so they could celebrate with him? Or maybe, my husband was too dazed to remember where it truly was? (More likely.) Either way, he was undeniably elated!

Imagine how Abraham and Sarah felt when they saw the promised child. After all their moments of agonizing doubt and taking matters into their own hands, God had at last come through. Yes, they had faith, but it had not been perfect. Sarah laughed when she was told she would have a child in a year, and she laughed again when she gave birth. She first laughed because she could not see how God was really going to make it happen. But God made it clear that nothing was too hard for him, and Sarah eventually enjoyed the fulfilling laughter of celebrating God's blessing.

All of us have faced or will face times of trials when we just can't seem to imagine how God will come through to help us. If you have never experienced such a trial, just wait, you will see his hand work. It is during those times that our faith is stretched. Of course, not all of us will enjoy a proverbial happy ending to these struggles, but through faith, God can and will use those difficulties to reveal his power and his grace in our lives.

In the Bible, Paul shares how he was given a painful physical problem to keep him from becoming too proud.

> *I begged the Lord three times to take this problem away from me. But he said to me, "My grace is enough for you. When you are weak, my power is made perfect in you." So I am very happy to brag about my weaknesses. Then Christ's power can live in me. For this reason I am happy when I have weaknesses, insults, hard times, sufferings, and all kinds of troubles for Christ. Because when I am weak, then I am truly strong.*

> (2 Corinthians 12:8-12, NCV)

The amazing part about this passage is it tells us that God's power is made "perfect" in our weaknesses. We might ask: *How does my weakness make God's power perfect?* All of us have weaknesses to deal with. We have sinful natures that hound us in our walk with the Lord. And yet, despite all our flaws and failings, God still uses our lives to glorify him. His grace is enough for us. In God's grace, he allows us to impact and to influence others despite our shortcomings, and sometimes even because of them. It is at those times that his power is made PERFECT in our weakness. No one can boast about his or her victories without giving glory to God who continues to use us.

Many of us have felt lonely at work, at school or in our neighborhoods, sometimes being the only Christians living in an unfair world, trying our best to stay committed to Jesus. We have tried our best to have faith in difficult situations, but nothing seems to change. We really want that certain something to happen, but it just doesn't seem like it will transpire. You might be like Sarah who waited and waited for a child but never had one. You might be single, waiting for the right man to come along, but none of them have been the right one for you.

I wonder how all of us would feel reading these same passages in the Bible about Sarah if she had given birth when she was forty years old instead of ninety—a little on the old side, but not too old. Would we marvel in the same way at God's glory in Isaac's birth? Would we laugh as heartily alongside Sarah at the birth of her child? Would we be as inspired by Abraham and Sarah's faith?

God had *his* timing. God had *his* plan. God knew what he was doing. His graciousness allowed the imperfect faith of Sarah to work in her life and throughout history to inspire even our hearts today.

Listen to me, you who pursue righteousness and who seek the Lord: Look to the rock from which you were cut and to the quarry from which you were hewn; Look to Abraham, your father and to Sarah, who gave you birth. When I called him he was but one, and I blessed him and made him many. The Lord will surely comfort Zion and will look with compassion on all her ruins, he will make her deserts like Eden, her wastelands like the garden of the Lord. Joy and gladness will be found in her, thanksgiving and the sound of singing.

(Isaiah 51:1-3, NIV)

In this passage, the prophet Isaiah makes a reference to Abraham and Sarah as an encouragement to the Israelites. At the time, the people of Israel had dwindled to a remnant. There were very few of them left. Yet these few people were seeking to do what was right. God was trying to remind them of how their father Abraham and their mother Sarah, who gave them birth, were but one. God was faithful, and he made them many. He told them how he would make their wastelands like Eden, a place of paradise, where joy and gladness would be found with thanksgiving and singing.

When I was a little girl, I had a maid who called me Princess and a butler who drove me everywhere. My life as a "princess" did not prepare me for the tough times ahead of me. I did not know what true suffering looked like after being pampered and served all my life. That changed when I began to live the life of a foreign missionary with my husband soon after we were married. When we first went to the mission field, different members from several congregations committed to support us financially through a program called the "Hawaiian Punch Can ministry". A family or household would put in their extra change daily into an empty juice can, or Hawaiian Punch can. At the end of each month, they would send the money to us. We were extremely grateful for the generosity of those Christians. However, some of the months, people would forget or have financial troubles and not send their support. As a result, we lived on the edge financially, but God always provided when we needed it the most.

Later, as missionaries to Japan, we faced not only financial challenges, but health ones as well. I was diagnosed with an aggressive form of lupus (Systemic Lupus Erythematosus) in 1991. I was so ill that doctors did not know what to do since lupus was incurable. Many Christians from around the world fasted and prayed for me during that time. One of our supporting churches raised extra money so that we could pay our hospital bills. I am forever thankful for those brothers and sisters who took out the time to pray and to sacrifice for me.

After that diagnosis, I went through years of holistic treatments. I was in a holding pattern—waiting for God to miraculously heal me and allow me to go into remission. There were months and months that I did not feel well and could not even take care of my little girls. For nearly two years, I was almost completely bedridden. My hair fell out. I suffered from infections constantly. I lost a lot of weight. I had joint and body pain everywhere. I suffered from coughing fits, because the lupus had attacked my lungs. I vomited many days from intense migraine headaches. During those years I was not able to serve the church in my former capacity, and as a result, I often felt hopeless, wondering if my life was a complete waste.

I remember asking my doctor what his goal for my treatments was. He replied by simply saying, "I'm going to get you well and in remission as soon as possible!" Now I didn't laugh like Sarah, but I did smile inwardly at his audacious proclamation. I could feel God saying to me, "Believe in me, Erica. I can do anything." But at the time, I did not have the same faith as the doctor. In fact, I battled with unbelief, doubt and discouragement.

In 1995, after several years of struggling through excruciatingly slow improvement, the doctor proclaimed me officially in remission. Hallelujah! I was so excited and happy to be free from the horrible effects of my disease. I laughed out loud when the doctor told me. I couldn't believe that after all that time, I was finally better again. I told Frank, and then we announced it to our little girls who could not stop jumping up and down on my bed with joy. My husband and I laughed again as we watched our girls celebrate. God gave me six wonderful years of remission before my illness became active again. But, thankfully, it has never returned with the same vengeance as before. I have been able to swim, ride my bike and stay very active in the church as a volunteer for the last few years while managing my condition.

In the passage from Isaiah above, God describes how he will look on his people with compassion and all Israel's ruins and deserts would become like Eden. He had a plan to bring joy and gladness to Israel again. It was an encouragement to the faithful few who struggled to seek God. Following God and striving to obey his commands is not an easy task. We are constantly tested through hardship and adversity. As the scriptures make it clear, few will make that decision to follow Jesus, because the way is narrow and few will find it (Matthew 7:13-14).

We know the end of this story with the Israelites. They overcame the tribulation of the times and remained faithful to God. *The ransomed of the Lord will return. They will enter Zion with singing; everlasting joy will crown their heads. Gladness and joy will overtake them, and sorrow and sighing will flee away.* (Isaiah 51:11, NIV) More than that, this passage is a prediction for a greater joy, which would include everlasting joy, gladness and no more sorrow. Do those words seem familiar? Yes, it's a wonderful preview of heaven.

Faith is so fragile in this world. It is easily crushed by disappointment, suffering and ordeals. In this life, our faith will be severely tested by Satan. He has no pity or compassion on us. He will push and push until we reach our very limits. Often, when Satan is challenging us, we search for evidence of God working in our lives. We fight to hold onto even a small thread of faith.

In those times, we want confirmation that what we are doing and what we believe in is making a difference. We want to *feel* victorious. We *yearn* to touch and experience what God can do in our lives. So we seek validation whether it is through answered prayers, fruit from our efforts or blessings from our good works. We look for signs. Sometimes there will be no proof. At times, there will be no results. That is why Sarah was frustrated—there were no results from years of trying.

There is no doubt in my mind that Abraham and Sarah tried very hard to have a child. It must have been an all-consuming desire and almost an obsession in Sarah's mind. Imagine month after month, year after year with no results. The years turned into decades. The decades turned into almost a century of waiting with no sign of a baby...until those angels appeared to Abraham when he was ninety-nine years old.

Faith cannot be measured by results. Faith cannot be measured by the amount of blessings in a person's life. Faith cannot be measured by what we have and don't have. Faith cannot be measured by how faultless we are. However, for each of us, our faith was sufficient to receive his grace. This is God's absolute grace.

> *He (Christ) redeemed us in order that the blessing given to Abraham might come to the Gentiles through Christ Jesus, so that **by faith** we might receive the promise of the Spirit.*
>
> (Galatians 3:14, NIV)

Having a child did not result from all of Sarah's many efforts. But it was rather through faith in the promise. Sarah finally surrendered to the plan of God and decided to completely believe that God would do as he said he would. *She* decided to believe alongside her husband and put one hundred percent of her trust into God.

> *Even when Sarah was too old to have children, she had faith that God would do what he had promised, and she had a son. Her husband Abraham was almost dead, but he became the ancestor of many people. In fact, there are as many of them as there are stars in the sky or grains of sand along the beach.*
>
> (Hebrews 11:11-12, CEV)

Sarah knew that she was too old, but she gave God every inch of her trust and faith at the age of ninety, as flawed as that trust and faith might have been.

Often, we can get frustrated with ourselves thinking that God doesn't work in our lives because we don't have enough faith. We berate ourselves for not getting what we want, when we want it, and blame ourselves for not having enough faith. I know that I have beaten myself up over and over for this, as most women probably do. Yet Jesus, the one who redeemed us, made it clear to his disciples that despite the fact they had so little faith, their measly faith, even as small as a mustard seed, would be able to move a mountain into the sea. He finished off by saying that nothing would be impossible for them (Matthew 17:20). Now that is encouraging!

So how much faith is enough faith? When it comes to measurements, Jesus provides us with only one. In other words, we just need to have faith—whether great or small. When she first laughed, Sarah's faith was small. Perhaps as small as a mustard seed? But you see, it was sufficient. God's grace does not measure our faith. God just wants us to have the faith that even in our weakest moments, he is at work in us.

Just understanding this kind of grace should make us rejoice and place our hope in God. We do not have to be bogged down by the disappointments of life, since we know that we will see the glory of God, now and forever. Perhaps there are things in this life that we will never have, but we know we can look forward to heaven and therefore have peace with God. At that time, we will laugh again—out loud and with overflowing joy—when we remember how much he has blessed our lives through his grace. Friends, let us be true daughters of Sarah.

 ## QUESTIONS FOR THE HEART

1. We women have always had to wait on God for something whether it's been for a husband, children or for a situation to change. It seems as though God makes us wait according to his timing and not ours. What are the things that you are still waiting for?

2. Read Psalm 37:1-7. Focus on the words: trust, take delight, commit your way, be still, and wait patiently. Are these words that describe your life right now? Pray through this psalm so that you can truly trust in the Lord to work through the challenges in your life right now.

3. Righteousness can still be achieved though our faith is not perfect. We may take matters into our own hands and try to control our lives, but we need to remember that God is in control. Read Psalm 27:1-30. Write down each description the psalmist uses to illustrate God. Decide today that you will allow him to take control over the areas of your life that you have no control over.

RAHAB: GOD'S GRACE FOR THE UNLOVED

God Loves the Unlovable

(Suggested Reading Joshua 2 & 6)

When I was eighteen years old, I took a trip to Japan with Pat Gempel, a mature and spiritual businesswoman who had become one of my early mentors in the faith. Pat encouraged me to read the Old Testament book of Esther during our trip. I was a brand new Christian at the time and very passionate about my faith. As I read about Esther, I learned many wonderful lessons. At the same time, I found myself becoming disheartened, because I realized that I was nothing like her. She was beautiful and talented—but most importantly, she was obedient, pure-hearted and a virgin. Those qualities pierced me like a knife. One morning, while Pat was in the adjacent bed reading her Bible, I interrupted her. I began to confess to Pat how sad I was that I was not at all like Esther.

Honestly, the part that saddened me the most was not being a virgin.

As the conversation progressed, Pat discerned the real issue and reassured me by saying, "Erica, you are a virgin. When you became a Christian, God washed away all your sins. In his eyes, you are pure and clean: a virgin. So when you get married, you can wear white with confidence, knowing that God has not only forgiven you, but that he has chosen to forget all your sins as well." Those words brought me so much comfort in God's grace. Until that moment, I hadn't fully understood God's forgiveness to be something so all-embracing and complete.

Only two and a half years after that conversation, Pat watched me walk down the aisle of the venerable Arlington Street Church in downtown Boston. As I approached my then-future husband, Frank, I was completely confident in wearing white, a virgin bride going to her groom. That was thirty years ago. I am still in love with him, and we have been faithful to one another throughout that time. I am so thankful to God for our marriage.

As women, we often feel unlovable. Secretly in our hearts, we think that if others really knew us, they wouldn't like us at all. We keep a part of ourselves hidden away so that no one will ever know how ugly we truly are. We erect walls and live within them, hoping that no one will ever see the truth. Those walls are thick and impenetrable to everyone, except to the rare few we dare let in. At one point, God came in and rescued us from our sins, breaking down the walls. Sadly, as the years go by, even as Christians we can rebuild the walls that were never meant to be raised up again.

Rahab was a prostitute. Of all the women that we would consider as most unlovable, it would probably be someone like her. She lived within the walls of Jericho (Joshua 2:15), hidden away but available to men who desired her services. The gates of Jericho were known to be impenetrable: once they were shut no one came in or went out (Joshua 6:1). Her location in the wall was perfect for Rahab's profession—on the outskirts of the community, but with access to her clients—away from nosy neighbors whose gossip ran rampant. Isolated from the rest of Jericho, she lived a life that was far from being pure and admirable.

Yet, God chose to have Rahab mentioned several times in the Bible, from the Old Testament to the New Testament. In fact, he chose her to star in the lineage of his own son, Jesus. It is interesting to note that she never lost her title: Rahab, the prostitute. Her reputation stuck with her through the centuries into the book of Hebrews. Perhaps God kept this title alongside her name to show all of us how much he loves the unlovable and how far his grace extends to those who decide to have faith in him.

Grace Transforms the Unlovable

Hebrews chapter 11 is often referred to as the "Faith Hall of Fame." Stalwart spiritual heroes such as Abraham and Moses are mentioned and praised for their faith. Just two women appear on this hallowed list. One is Sarah, the mother of faith to all of God's people.

The other?

Rahab.

Imagine being placed side by side with a woman like Sarah in the "Faith Hall of Fame"—especially if you had lived a sinful life like Rahab. But despite her foreign birth and way of life, God accepted her and received her as one of *his* people. She was rewarded for believing in God and protecting his people with her life. This honor was given to her because of one decision in her life, and as a result, she was commended as a woman of faith.

Did she stop being a prostitute? Did she finally renounce her sinful life? Was she willing to sell everything and start over? She probably did all these things and even more, but that is not the focus of the scriptures. The story of Rahab is all about the faith of an unlovable person—a reject of society.

It's a story of how God's grace works.

> *But God showed his great love for us by sending Christ to die for us while we were still sinners. And since we have been made right in God's sight by the blood of Christ, he will certainly save us from God's condemnation. For since our friendship with God was restored by the death of his Son while we were still his enemies, we will certainly be saved through the life of his Son.*
>
> (Romans 5:8-10, NLT)

When someone mentions grace, the above scripture is often read. But do we really appreciate and comprehend its true and incredible meaning? According to this passage, we were enemies of God—rejects in God's eyes and unlovable because of our sins. We were sinners who did not deserve to be loved. How easy it is for us to see the sins of others, but do we see the reality of our own failings? Jesus died for us, when we were morally polluted, spiritually detestable and full of evil. He died when we were *his enemies.* God sacrificed his one and only Son when we were objects of wrath (Ephesians 2:3).

What is an object of wrath? Think about how you would feel toward someone who murdered your child. That person would certainly be an object of wrath to you. If you cannot imagine someone murdering your child, imagine your mother or father being brutally killed. Could we, as human beings, ever sacrifice for that enemy? How easy would it be for us to forgive such a person? Could we even stand to be around that person, much less die for him?

Yet God uses the murder of his Son, with us as the murderers, to be the instrument and conduit for our eternal salvation. As John said, "For God so loved the world that he gave his only Son...." (John 3:16, NIV)

That concept does not make sense to the world. In fact, Paul writes how the message of the cross is "foolishness to those who are perishing." (1 Corinthians 1:18)

Decide by Faith not Fear

Rahab took a chance through faith. She made a crucial decision to save the two spies who came to Jericho. She put her life at risk, sacrificing everything for these two strangers in whose God she had put her absolute faith.

> *...[T]he king of Jericho was told, "Look! Some of the Israelites have come here tonight to spy out the land." So the king of Jericho sent this message to Rahab: "Bring out the men who came to you and entered your house, because they have come to spy out the whole land." But the woman had taken the two men and hidden them. She said, "Yes, the men came to me, but I did not know where they had come from. At dusk, when it was time to close the city gate, the men left. I don't know which way they went. Go after them quickly. You may catch up with them." (But she had taken them up to the roof and hidden them under the stalks of flax she had laid out on the roof.)*
>
> (Joshua 2:4-6, NIV)

Imagine if a king sent you a message commanding you to hand over your guests, but instead of obeying, you did the exact opposite. How would you feel?

What a frightening position to be in! Rahab put aside her fears, resolved to trust in the God of Israel, and decided to disobey her king. Rahab's deep faith gave her the strength to protect the two Israelites, knowing that she could be imprisoned and even killed for hiding them from the king. The guards who came to her home searched the whole house, only to come out empty-handed. While probably shaking with fear, she lied to the guards who came to her home and then advised them to chase after the men to the fords of the Jordan, sending them on a wild goose chase.

When the king's men left, she went up to the roof to check on her new friends. She did not waver in disbelief but was reinforced in her faith for having done what was right. She had convictions about the God of Israel and what he could do to save her and her family. So she put everything on the altar before the God of heaven and earth.

> *Now before they lay down, she came up to them on the roof, and said to the men, "I know that the LORD has given you the land, and that the terror of you has fallen on us, and that all the inhabitants of the land have melted away before you. For we have heard how the LORD dried up the water of the Red Sea before you when you came out of Egypt, and what you did to the two kings of the Amorites who were beyond the Jordan, to Sihon and Og, whom you utterly destroyed. "When we heard it, our hearts melted and no courage remained in any man any longer because of you; for the LORD your God, He is God in heaven above and on earth beneath.*
>
> (Joshua 2:8-11, NASB)

Rahab believed in a God that she had never personally seen or experienced. That is amazing faith. Before she had ever learned about the God of Israel, she was calling him "Lord". She was the one recounting the miracles of God to the spies rather than the other way around. Then, she made a confession of faith saying, "The Lord your God, he is God in heaven above and on earth beneath." She put her complete faith in him even though she had not yet personally experienced his power and had only heard about him from a distance. Of all the people in the city who had heard the same stories as she did, Rahab was the only one willing to put her complete faith in the God of Israel. Her faith was what transformed her.

Before marrying my husband, I was engaged to another man who wined and dined me as well as bought me expensive gifts. He was several years older than me and extremely wealthy. I was completely enamored of and in love with him until I realized that he had been cheating on me with several women. Instead of breaking up with him, however, I built a wall to protect myself from being hurt, all the while hoping that I could somehow get him to change by being a "better" fiancé. Meanwhile, he kept professing his love for me and continued to reassure me that all those "other" women were meaningless flings. He told me that I was the only one who really mattered to him. I hated myself for forgiving him over and over again. I was not confident enough in myself to confront him. Many times, I thought there was something wrong with me.

It was not until I began to learn about the Bible and its amazing truth that I was able to stand up against what my fiancé was doing in our relationship. I also gained the courage to tell him that I wanted a pure relationship with godly standards. Through God's power, I acquired the conviction to live according to God's Word rather than by my feelings. I changed and started to walk by faith on a transformational path, which then enabled me to keep all my following dating relationships pure.

This same faith also saves each of us. No matter what we have done in the past, God can transform us into new creations in Christ. (2 Corinthians 5:17) God works his power through our faith, and he will do so much more for those of us who continue to believe.

Don't Go Back into the Wall

From the perspective of the people of Jericho, Rahab was a *nobody*, a person of no significance. She was unworthy to be considered a "normal" citizen of the city and lived in the shadows of the negligible part of Jericho. Her life, her domicile, her job, and her family were literally on the fringe of society—she was an unloved and disrespected woman. Who would want to be friends with a woman of her reputation? Who would be proud to be a part of her family? Who would sacrifice their status to associate with a prostitute?

Dear sisters, no matter who we were, where we have come from and what we have done, God is willing to accept us as we are. We might have lived a life similar to Rahab, giving our lives over to men, all the while hating ourselves, but hoping to find love in our desperation. We felt the emptiness. We hurt deep inside but didn't fight it, because there was no hope in us for something better. It was not until we found true love in Christ that we were able to turn around and live a new life.

But as the years have gone by, have the old insecurities returned to haunt you? Maybe you have hit obstacles in your life or have failed in discouraging ways. Perhaps the love of your life has walked out on you, leaving you all alone. Maybe you have lost your dream job and have not been able to find another one. Or are you mourning the tragic and painful loss of yet another loved one? Perhaps you feel defeated and unloved—even unloved by your God who you feel has let you down. In the midst of such disappointment, do you find yourself erecting walls and living in them again?

Satan loves playing mind-games with us. He wants us to go back to our old ways of thinking. He wants us to believe that we cannot change. He does his best to manipulate us into thinking we are worthless. He can even use people we love to make us feel that we are never going to be good enough. The walls we construct are there because we have decided to believe his lies rather than continuing to have faith in God.

If adversity or disappointment has caused you to respond like this, it is time to fight back! Satan messes with our thinking. He enjoys the pain that each of us feel when we rebuild those thick walls and choose to once again live within their isolation. Satan wants us to forget that we are precious and treasured by God. He tries to make us forget all that God gave up for our salvation.

Ask yourself: Would God sacrifice his Son for someone he didn't love? Of course not. You see, even at our worst and most sinful times, God looked at you and me as the "apple of his eye."

For the LORD's portion is his people, Jacob his allotted inheritance. In a desert land he found him, in a barren and howling waste. He shielded him and cared for him; he guarded him as the apple of his eye, like an

eagle that stirs up its nest and hovers over its young, that spreads its
wings to catch them and carries them on its pinions.

(Deuteronomy 32:9-11, NIV)

An eagle stirs up its nest so that its young will take flight. This natural procedure forces its young to literally fall out of the nest so they will learn to spread their wings and fly. However, if one of the young birds fails to fly, the eagle will not allow it to fall and die. Instead, it will dive down and catch its young in the pinions of its wings. That is how God shielded and protected the Israelites at a time when they were complaining and grumbling.

You have seen what I did to the Egyptians, and how I bore you on eagles'
wings and brought you to Myself.

(Exodus 19:4 AMP)

After having escaped the clutches of their cruel Egyptian masters, the struggling Israelites were longing to go back to Egypt—back into slavery. God had split the Red Sea for them. He had guided them through the desert with a cloud by day and a pillar of fire by night. The cloud shielded them from the hot sun. The fire warmed them in the cool of the desert. Their sandals never wore out in the wilderness—for sandals not to fall apart after forty years is quite remarkable even for us in modern times. They had manna and quail provided from the sky. They didn't lack water—they were in a desert land, but they had plenty to drink.

In short, God carried them in the pinions of his wings to the Promised Land.

Rahab had heard about all these miracles and decided to trust in the God of Israel. She did not let the world influence her. She was ready to push forward and to not look back. She was done with living in the wall. She was ready to step out on faith and to believe that this God would accept her as she was— unlovable, unworthy and insignificant. She was also prepared to go the next step by renouncing her past, fighting back her fears, and leaving behind her reputation in order to follow the God who would guide her life.

Now many of us may have never lived a "Rahab" life, but we have all done many sinful things all the same. We have cheated, lied, slandered and hurt others. And although we may have accepted God's grace and promise of a new start, we can find ourselves once again doing or feeling things we thought we had given up. As a result, we again feel shame and guilt. And yet, the message of grace is that no matter where we have come from, we can overcome the negative voices that twist our memories and thoughts to convince us we are contemptible, unworthy, or unforgivable in God's sight. These kinds of thoughts are paralyzing and destructive. Even the world recognizes negative thinking is detrimental—and also that faithful thinking is powerfully good.

Doctors say people who have faith and hope heal faster and far more effectively than those who do not. In a study of heart surgery patients, a group of researchers from Duke University Medical Center in Durham, North Carolina, actually discovered that those who relied on prayer and spirituality were three times **less likely** to die within six months following their surgery than those who had no deep faith.[2]

In other words, having no faith and hope can even shorten our physical life expectancy. It certainly is damaging to our emotional and spiritual health. How can we be healed of those pessimistic and faithless voices? How can we get rid of the walls that surround our hearts? God gives us the medicine: faith. Our confidence does not need to come from ourselves but from God. Just as Rahab put her trust in God, we can find strength through trusting in him. This doesn't mean that all our problems will magically go away, but it does mean we can overcome and be healed.

Look at what Jesus did when Satan tried to play mind-games with him. He used Peter, his best friend, to confuse him. But Jesus did not sit back and take it. He did not allow it to consume him—instead he fought back.

Jesus turned and said to Peter, "Get behind me, Satan! You are a stumbling block to me; you do not have in mind the things of God, but the things of men.

(Matthew 16:23, NIV)

One of my daughters used to have night terrors when she was a child. I told her to command those monsters and bad people that came into her dreams to go away in the name of Jesus. So she would shout out in her dreams, "In the name of Jesus, I command you to go away!" It took her a few times before she would remember to do that, but, over time, she stopped having nightmares. Even as an adult now, she does the same thing and the evil people leave from her dreams.

Before those destructive thoughts take root into our psyche, let's take command of them. Jesus' power works. But it takes faith. We don't have to go back to the old wall that we used to live in to protect ourselves. God is there for us, and he will catch us when we fall. We need to replace Satan's accusations with God's powerful proclamations:

You are lovable—so lovable to God that he gave everything for you
(Romans 8:32).

You are special—so special that God chose you to be his daughter
(Ephesians 1:11).

You are important—so treasured that God sacrificed his Son for you
(John 3:16).

You are precious—so valued that he will be with you through the best and
worst of times (Isaiah 43:4).

You are cherished—a prized possession that of all the people in the world,
he picked you to be holy (Deuteronomy 14:2).

You are worthy—because you have suffered for his name
(2 Thessalonians 1:5).

> *Summing it all up, friends, I'd say you'll do best by filling your minds and meditating on things true, noble, reputable, authentic, compelling, gracious—the best, not the worst; the beautiful, not the ugly; things to praise, not things to curse. Put into practice what you learned from me, what you heard and saw and realized. Do that, and God, who makes everything work together, will work you into his most excellent harmonies.*
>
> (Philippians 4:8-9, The Message)

Being Open to New Paths

God opened up a new path for Rahab's life. It was a path to the unknown. This new life was going to be nothing like the one she had been living. It was a time for change or *death*. She had to make the most crucial decision of her life—a choice between life and death, both for herself and her family. For some reason, God placed the two spies in her home, giving her an open door. She did not give in to fear but decided to trust and obey.

> *"Our lives for your lives!" the men assured her. "If you don't tell what we are doing, we will treat you kindly and faithfully when the LORD gives us the land." So she let them down by a rope through the window, for the house she lived in was part of the city wall.*
>
> (Joshua 2:14-15, NIV)

There was an exchange of trust— "our lives for your lives," said the men. So Rahab lowered the rope from the wall and helped the men to escape. She stepped out of her comfort zone and helped two strangers who could have broken their promise. She did not know what would eventually happen. She had no idea how she would be treated, even if they spared her life. Besides, they were the enemy, were they not? All she knew was that she would trust in the God of Israel to give her a better life.

Most of us ladies would never trust strangers nor would we want to change our lives for the unknown. We don't like to get out of our comfort zones. And if we could control life and keep it stable, most of us would gladly take that option. We don't like surprises, but sometimes, we are faced with open doors and opportunities, which stretch us beyond what is comfortable.

On the other hand, there are also a few of us who like adventure and challenge, but it can get old after a while. Why? Because adventures and challenges can wear us out both physically and emotionally as well as mess up our "groove."

As for me, I don't like change. If it were up to me, I would love to live in one place and stay there for the rest of my life. Don't get me wrong. I like adventure too, but in moderation—a trip or two a year to some exotic place would be wonderful. But in everyday life, I prefer to have my little nest in place.

God, however, has worked on me for the last thirty years of my life to get that "settler" mentality out of my system. I have lived on three continents, in five countries and nine cities during the years I have been a Christian. In addition to that, God gave me a husband who is a "pioneer." My husband loves to live in new places every few years. He loves to meet new people and experience wild and crazy adventures — whether it is to start a church in communist Cambodia or to preach in the trains of the Paris subways—he is always looking for new challenges to call his faith higher.

Meanwhile, I follow along and get excited…the majority of the time. Like I said, I would rather live a peaceful life with daily routines. Although I do enjoy challenges at times, it is not my nature to go looking for them. Nonetheless, God has put me in situations to stretch my faith, so that I can keep maturing in my walk with him. I praise God for my husband who helps me to keep growing to be my best for Him.

Rahab was not a "settler." She was a pioneer, ready to do what God called her to do. She welcomed the change and the new path set before her. She pushed past her fears and was able to see life differently and gain confidence. She embraced the opportunity that lay ahead, not worrying about the issues that can often engulf women. She did not allow herself to be overcome with anxiety and concern such as: *What about my house? Where will I live? What if I don't like where I'm moving to? What about my job? Who will hire me and what will I do in the future? Where will the money come from? Will I be able to make new friends?*

Rahab remained faithful to the oath she had made to the spies. She did not waver; otherwise, again, it would have probably been mentioned in the scriptures. As a result, she not only saved herself but her family as well.

Each of us will have various opportunities and new paths open to us at different points in our lives. Yet we can have a negative attitude toward those open doors. Instead of facing them with faith, we can become angry, resentful and bitter. Rather than seeing God's hand working to give us a chance to strengthen our faith or to spread our wings, we can interpret the open doors as punishment or discipline. But God does not work in this way. He wants us to grow, to be our best, and to live our lives to the fullest. We often deprive ourselves of the blessings that come through such opportunities because of our stubborn attitudes.

After the death of my mother, I remember being asked to move from San Francisco to help lead a small mission church in Tokyo, Japan. It was a scary move for me; especially after suddenly losing my mother, it was hard to leave friends who could help me through the grieving process. It had only been four months since my mother's passing. I did not see this as a great opportunity, but rather as a test from God. I was not excited about the prospect of moving to a new country, a new city and speaking a new language. Meanwhile, my pioneer husband was beside himself. His blood was pumping. His feet were skipping around everywhere he went, and his eyes sparkled with anticipation just thinking about the opportunity.

After moving to Japan, watching my husband helped me to change my attitude. He would come home each night and tell me about his adventures on the subway, in the stores and on the streets as he met new people and tried out all the new words he was learning. Although I spoke a different dialect, I, at least, understood what people were saying. But Frank was starting from zero in learning Japanese. His desire to learn and to adjust to the new environment inspired me. Before I knew it, I was just as excited as my husband and ended up making many new friends who helped me over the next fifteen years of my life.

I saw God's grace working as I dealt with the myriad challenges of culture shock, mourning for my mother, adjusting to new people, settling in a different home and making many cultural faux-pas. I learned to laugh at myself even as people chuckled at my mistakes. I grew in my faith more than I could have ever imagined and reached a new level of conviction. Those years in Asia changed my life forever. Despite the ways I dragged my feet at first, God was gracious in allowing me to be used. Even though I made lots of mistakes, I also learned through them. God took a young woman and allowed me to mature into his instrument.

One of my closest friends, Barri Lusk, moved to Bangkok, Thailand around the same time to be a missionary. She is a Louisiana girl who still has her accent to this day. She had never lived outside the United States, but was so excited to move to a foreign country. She moved to Thailand with her husband, John, and a small baby, not knowing the language, the culture or the religion.

What amazed me about Barri was her desire to serve God. For her, this was the opportunity and blessing of a lifetime. She went to Bangkok with a faith and zeal to serve God. She was ready for change. She was eager for adventure. She welcomed all the challenges with trust. She worked hard to learn the language, to understand the culture and to befriend people who were entirely different from her.

The Lusks have left an impact in the Bangkok church that lasts to this day. They converted millionaires, poor people, influential people and needy people.

They helped prostitutes, homosexuals and transvestites. They encountered situations that do not exist in the States. Yet, they conquered all those difficulties with God's power.

Even though she has since moved back to the U.S., Barri speaks fluent Thai to this day. Her love for Thailand remains in her spirit. She took this opportunity and viewed it as God's grace—taking her to the ends of the earth, far past her comfort zone and beyond what she had ever experienced before. As a result, she grew into a beautiful woman of God, not only outwardly, but especially inwardly, full of faith and a positive attitude toward all changes in her life.

God's grace molds us, teaches us and stretches us. It is never there to crush us. We, however, sometimes crush ourselves with our own negativity and bitterness. He calls each of us to have greater faith, deeper convictions and a more mature attitude toward him. By his grace, God will use us despite ourselves. He desires to see us develop an eager attitude with fortitude and determination.

Just like Rahab, who chose to trust even when she could have doubted, we, too, can put our trust in God. He wants all of us to pour out everything for him so that he can work through the opportunities, challenges and changes in our lives. In this way, we can march out with confidence to the new paths and places while we follow the path that he takes us on. We are not alone when we launch towards unknown horizons. God tells us in the book of Psalm:

> *I will instruct you and teach you in the way which you should go; I will counsel you with My eye upon you.*
>
> (Psalm 32:8, NASB)

> *For this God is our God forever and ever; he will be our guide even to the end.*
>
> (Psalm 48:14, NIV)

Letting Go

Letting go of the past, of regret, of sin, of fears, of hurts and of addictions allows us to live unburdened lives. It is also just as important to learn to let go of loved ones, such as our grown children, as they move on—and sometimes away from us—in life. "Letting go" is a part of healing. Healing finally takes place when we can make crucial decisions to let go of the *yokes* that weigh down our spirits. Anxiety, worry, sadness and hopelessness are all encumbrances that damage and bruise our faith—sometimes to the point of no return. Look at the world. To dull the pain of the past, the concerns of this world, or loss of relationships, people turn to drugs, alcohol, and sadly, even suicide.

Jesus promised us a life to the full—not without many problems—but one full of hope.

> *Come to me, all you who are weary and burdened, and I will give you rest. Take my yoke upon you and learn from me, for I am gentle and humble in heart, and you will find rest for your souls. For my yoke is easy and my burden is light.*
>
> (Matthew 11:28-30, NIV)

A **yoke** is a wooden beam, which is used between a pair of oxen to allow them to pull a load (oxen always work in pairs).[3] In the same way, life is full of burdens and problems, and when we carry them around, we almost always drag someone else along with us. Whether we mean for it to happen or not, the yoke that is placed on our necks also gets connected to the ones we love the most in this life. So often, our personal pain ends up hurting those closest to us. All the while, we allow these heavy loads to hold us down and immobilize us in our faith.

Jesus tells us to take *his yoke* upon us. Jesus wants to pull the cart with us—alongside us—so that we can find rest for our souls. He wants us to learn from him, because he is gentle and humble in heart. You see a pair of oxen can pull many hundreds of pounds of grain, dirt and other materials. But far too often, we don't reach out to Jesus, and we make ourselves pull countless burdens that we were never meant to carry alone. The yoke of this life can become unbearable and even oppressive.

> *When the seventh day came, they (the Israelites) got up early and marched around the city this same way but seven times—yes, this day they circled the city seven times. On the seventh time around the priests blew the trumpets and Joshua signaled the people, "Shout!—God has*

given you the city! The city and everything in it is under a holy curse and offered up to God. "Except for Rahab the harlot—she is to live, she and everyone in her house with her, because she hid the agents we sent.

(Joshua 6:15-17, The Message)

Imagine Rahab waiting faithfully in her home while the Jews marched around the city for six days. Then, finally, on the seventh day, the Israelite army rushed into the city as the mighty walls crumbled. She heard Joshua shout out her name. "You can kill everyone in the city…but not Rahab!"

How would you feel as your city is attacked by a mighty army–but then hearing the leader of the whole Israelite army specifically commanding not to harm you or your family? That alone would make anyone feel special.

At the same time, notice how Joshua describes Rahab: "the harlot!" In front of the people who were about to become her new nation. How embarrassing! On the very brink of a new start, a new chapter, and a new beginning, Rahab is reminded of her sordid past. How would she respond?

We also have a choice, just like Rahab. We can hold onto to the burdens in life that God never meant for us to carry, or we can give our burdens over to him. Letting go is a part of accepting God's grace. You see, often many of us have a nasty tape recorder in our brains. It plays back all the scenarios of what should not have been. It beats us up over and over again, robbing us of our faith and minimizing the grace of God. How can any human being live under the burden of all the mistakes and sins she has committed? We can become like the world by either hardening our hearts morally or numbing our pain in harmful ways. Or we can accept the grace of God and live with faith like Rahab.

Rahab accepted God's grace, so her reputation of being a prostitute did not matter anymore. Instead of allowing it to become a burden in her life, she chose to allow her "title" to bring glory and honor to God. She did not shout from the wall, "No, Joshua, you're mistaken. I'm not going to be a harlot anymore. I'm changing my ways once I get out of here! So please let everyone know that I'm just Rahab and leave out the part about being a prostitute!"

When we allow the past to burden us, we put ourselves behind an imaginary wall in an effort to protect ourselves, but it can be self-destructive, trapping our souls inside. We become the victims of our own millstones, which we tie around our own necks. This should not be. God gives us the power to be released from those ugly snares. Rahab lived with the reputation of being a prostitute for the rest of her life. Even to this day, when we study about her in the scriptures, she is known as "Rahab the prostitute," even though she remained faithful to her husband for many years afterward. She, however, did not allow this to immobilize her, but recognized that it brought glory to God.

For years I had put a burden on myself that not many people knew about. Around the time my mother killed herself, I was one of the last people to spend time with her. She had flown all the way out to San Francisco to see me and to get help. During that week, we talked and shared, but it did not seem to help her, because she would not let go of certain burdens in her life. The night after she left, she took her life.

What was my burden? I thought that I had said something wrong resulting in her death. I felt I had exacerbated the problem rather than helping to save her. The guilt was so heavy at times that it would immobilize me: in my faith, in my confidence and in my trust in God. I kept thinking to myself that if I couldn't save my mother, how can I help anyone else? I kept beating myself up over and over again. Although the self-torture abated at times, it was always there for many years, until I was finally able to let go.

A few years after she died, I sat in a hotel room one day and wrote a long letter to my mother with my feelings inside. It took hours. After finishing the letter, I lit it with a match inside a garbage can and prayed to God that I would finally be freed from my prison. I believe that God freed me at that moment, because I have never gone back there again. My husband has often said that suffering is like a knife. We can grab it by the blade and let it continue to hurt us, or we can grab it by handle and use it.

This experience and this pain in my life have now become a tool in my ministry. It is no longer a burden that I secretly drag around in my heart or that weakens my faith. I have been able to relate with the pain of others and to help them to heal. I no longer hide behind my walls of secrets and try to "look good" to those outside. God has used this experience to see his grace more clearly.

I have had other women unburden themselves by confessing "secret" sins to me. When I asked them to tell their husbands or their children, they looked at me like I was from a different planet. Telling me had helped to take off some of the weight, but these secrets were extremely serious, and they feared they would jeopardize their families and their carefully constructed but fragile lives. They not only lived with guilt, but they could not let go and move on.

Dear friends, what secret burdens do you bear that weigh you down today? They are too heavy, and it is unnecessary for you to bear them alone. Many times your situation may not change or cannot be changed—but our hearts can be different. Rahab let go of her old life. She did not allow it to plague her and torture her in any way in her new life. It did not change anything about who she had been, but her perspective changed. And she acted on her faith in God by letting go and moving forward.

> *You see that a person is justified by what he does and not by faith alone. In the same way, was not even Rahab the prostitute considered righteous for what she did when she gave lodging to the spies and sent them off in a different direction? As the body without the spirit is dead, so faith without deeds is dead.*
>
> (James 2:24-26, NIV)

That day in the hotel did not change anything about the circumstances in my life, nor did it bring back my mother from the dead in some miraculous way. But my heart was unbound, freed of the burden of guilt, ready to move forward to help others. I decided to act on my faith. In fact, after that, I was inspired by God's Spirit to begin a ministry for mothers in the church. This ministry became a great instrument for helping older women to become Christians, and all of them adopted me as their daughter. God gave me new mothers, a hundred times over.

Real faith takes action. Rahab acted on her faith by saving the spies, warning her family, and then making them wait with her until the Israelites attacked.

> *By faith the prostitute Rahab, because she welcomed the spies, was not killed with those who were disobedient.*
>
> (Hebrews 11:31, NIV)

Do you need to let go? By faith, we all can! God doesn't want us to have our hands glued around the padlocks of our prison, keeping him from opening the cell door. We can pry our fingers off, one by one. We can learn to live by faith and not by sight, just like Rahab. We can be freed from the burdens that plague our lives. We can be listed in heaven's "Faith Hall of Fame" by making the decision to believe and no longer doubt.

> *Therefore, since we are surrounded by such a great cloud of witnesses, let us throw off everything that hinders and the sin that so easily entangles, and let us run with perseverance the race marked out for us. Let us fix our eyes on Jesus, the author and perfecter of our faith, who for the joy set before him endured the cross, scorning its shame, and sat down at the right hand of the throne of God. Consider him who endured such opposition from sinful men, so that you will not grow weary and lose heart.*
>
> (Hebrews 12:1-3, NIV)

 QUESTIONS FOR THE HEART

1. Do you hide who you really are because you feel as though no one could love you as you are? Take time out to write down names of at least two spiritual women who can help you in areas of your life that you hide from others. Pray for them to have the wisdom to help you.

2. Satan loves to play mind-games with us. He wants us to think negatively about ourselves. Read Philippians 4:8-9 three times out loud. Allow the words to sink inside your heart so that faithlessness will not crowd out the good that you have inside of you.

3. Letting go of the past can be difficult. The memories can become yokes around our necks. Are you accepting God's grace in your life? During you prayer time today, ask God to help you to accept his grace once and for all. Decide today that God's grace is more powerful than all our mistakes. Let those yokes go and accept His grace in your life.

Chapter 5

DEBORAH: RAISED UP THROUGH GRACE

(Suggested Reading: Judges 4 & 5)

Not all of us are natural leaders. Not all of us will be asked to lead large numbers of people. Not all of us feel confident standing before a crowd and giving a speech. If it were our choice, some of us would prefer to be in the audience and cheer on the leader and never have to be the one behind the podium. For those who can totally relate to this, you are not alone. Moses was afraid and wanted his brother to do all the talking. Jeremiah made his age an excuse and told God that he was too young to preach to the Israelites. Saul hid among the baggage when God called him to be the king of Israel. Jonah tried to run away from God so that he would not have to warn the Ninevites.

Answering the Call of God

At one point or another, all of us will be called by God to take leadership in some form. It may be in a small way when you are with your girlfriends who are slandering one of your friends behind her back, and you know you should say something. It may be in a greater way when one of your relatives is going through a huge crisis, and you are the one that he or she chooses to ask for help. It may be in an even more significant role when a church leader pulls you aside and asks you to take a leadership position in a ministry. Whatever the circumstance, it is by the grace of God that he calls us to take leadership in some form.

Why do we become frightened when God calls us? Are we afraid of failure? Is it our timidity that holds us back? How can we fight against the insecurity that affects our ability to respond to God? When we have the perspective that God is the one that is calling us, it is easier to respond, though it might still be challenging. At the same time, Satan wants us to be humanistic in our thinking. He tries to make us look at our limitations. He deceives us with, "Why me?"

In the Old Testament book of Judges, Deborah was chosen by God to be a judge (a leader) for Israel. After Ehud, the former judge died, the Israelites had done evil in the sight of the Lord, and God caused the Israelites to be cruelly oppressed by Jabin, the king of Canaan (Judges 4:3). At the time, Israel was in such distress and subjugation that the roads were too dangerous to use. The situation had become so unbearable for the Israelites that the Bible says that there was no village life until Deborah rose up (Judges 5:7-8).

Finally, the Israelites called out to the Lord in humility and repentance. God, being a gracious God, responded with a plan to defeat the Canaanites and regain Israel's freedom. Through Deborah, he told Barak, son of Abinoam, to lure Jabin's army into battle so that they could be conquered. But Barak refused to go unless Deborah went with him (Judges 4:8).

Barak appears to be imprisoned by his own humanistic and fearful thinking. He seems to ask: "Why me?" Despite receiving God's command and the promise to bless him with victory, Barak was not willing to attack if Deborah was not with him. According to scripture, this reluctance deprived him of honor from God.

"Why me?" is often a natural question, and can also be a mark of humility. The apostle Paul felt he was unworthy of the calling he had received from God and felt as though he should not have been called an apostle (1 Corinthians 15:9). He knew without a doubt it was not because of his incredible talents or abilities that he was chosen, but rather by the grace of God.

But by the grace of God I am what I am, and his grace to me was not without effect. No, I worked harder than all of them—yet not I, but the grace of God that was with me.

(I Corinthians 15:10, NIV)

Later in Paul's life he told Timothy that he was the worst of sinners.

The grace of our Lord was poured out on me abundantly, along with the faith and love that are in Christ Jesus. Here is a trustworthy saying that deserves full acceptance: Christ Jesus came into the world to save sinners—of whom I am the worst. But for that very reason I was shown mercy so that in me, the worst of sinners, Christ Jesus might display his unlimited patience as an example for those who would believe on him and receive eternal life.

(I Timothy 1:14-16, NIV)

It is godly to humbly acknowledge our unworthiness to be used by God. However, many of us fall into the trap of thinking that since we are not "good enough," we doubt that God *can* use us. Paul was convinced that he was the worst of sinners, but this did not stop him from giving his best to God. Instead, Paul worked harder than all of the other apostles. He said this effort was not from him—it was the grace of God working in him. In the same way, it is by the grace of God that we are called to have a certain role in his church or in society. We may not be perfectly talented or we may lack experience in the area in which we are called to serve, but we can grow to fit the task to which God calls us.

Then Deborah said to Barak, "Go! This is the day the LORD has given Sisera into your hands. Has not the LORD gone ahead of you?" So Barak went down Mount Tabor, followed by ten thousand men. At Barak's advance, the LORD routed Sisera and all his chariots and army by the sword, and Sisera abandoned his chariot and fled on foot. But Barak pursued the chariots and army as far as Harosheth Haggoyim. All the troops of Sisera fell by the sword; not a man was left.

(Judges 4:14-16, NIV)

Note that God did not take away the victory because of Barak's lack of confidence. He was still able to rout Jabin's army. All the troops commanded by Sisera fell by the sword and no survivors were left. It was a *complete* victory for the Lord. The good news is that if God can use Paul, the "worst of sinners," to help countless people come to faith in Christ, then God was certainly able to use an insecure Barak to subdue the Canaanites. There is nothing that is impossible with God (Luke 1:37).

So: what can one man or woman do? Each can do anything that God has purposed for him or her to do. It doesn't matter how young or old, talented or untalented, smart or average we are.

Why Deborah? The Bible does not give us an impressive list of her personal academic or professional credentials. We do not know her family background—whether she was from royalty or related to the past judges of Israel. But we do know that there was a need in Israel—a need for someone to take the lead.

While we lived in Japan, one woman that I grew to respect very deeply was Shizue Iwanaga. Her younger son had a tragic accident while cliff diving, rendering him paralyzed from the neck down. He was just nineteen years old at the time, and due to his injuries, he had to live at home for many years under his mother's devoted care. Amazingly, during that time, her son studied the Bible, changed his life, and became a Christian. Encouraged by his transformation, Shizue also began to read the Bible and to attend church with her son. She eventually made Jesus Lord of her own life. This wonderful decision, however, did not end the hardships she faced.

Shizue continued to take care of her son well into her sixties. She held firmly to her faith despite the exhausting physical challenges of going to church, being opposed by her non-Christian husband for her faith, and being criticized by other relatives as well. Even as a new Christian, she overcame the opposition she faced and lived out a faith that eventually affected her entire family. She persevered and worked tirelessly to serve them. As a result, her older son and his wife were also converted to Christ. Several years later, Shizue's grandson also became a Christian. Everyone in their family and in their church praised God when her younger son married a faithful Christian woman. That couple has since given Shizue yet another grandchild! Through his grace, God used this faithful, unassuming and hardworking woman to impact several generations of her family.

Life does not hand out a "perfect" situation to any Christian. In Shizue's case, she had to overcome one difficult circumstance after another. If it wasn't her son's condition, it was opposition from her husband. If it wasn't her family's criticism, it was her own fatigue that burdened her. But she never gave up. She endured the challenges not just over the months, but over the years. God used a sweet and humble woman to show God's incredible power through her life.

God will call each of us at certain points of our lives. Most of the time, it will be during inconvenient circumstances—as single mothers, as working mothers with small children, as a student finishing up a PhD, as a single professional just starting out in a career, or even during a traumatic divorce. God has a way of choosing moments when we feel the least equipped or ready in order to reveal his own power in our lives. All this helps us to see that it is not our ability or strength that causes the miracles, but rather the wonderful grace and love of God. And when the victory comes, we can never say that we did it ourselves, but that God did it all.

God's Gracious Plans Include Us All

We may have many ideas about what our lives should be like and what our futures should resemble, but we are obviously not in control of the events in our lives—not in the least. On the other hand, the Lord is in control, and he has his purposes for each of our lives. *Many are the plans in a man's (woman's) heart, but it is the Lord's purpose that prevails.* (Proverbs 19:21, NIV)[4]

God's plans and purpose are like a giant jigsaw puzzle. There are billions of pieces—almost seven billion to be more exact, and each piece is essential to the grand design. Some of the pieces have but one color or one purpose. Some of the pieces have a myriad of shades and colors with lots of curves and edges. But not one piece is more important than the rest. All of them are crucial to the entire pattern. So it is with each of our lives, not one person is less essential or more important, because every life is crucial to maintaining the balance of God's creation.

What we often imagine as being the right or perfect plan may not be a part of God's plans. Remember, God can thwart a whole nation of people. He can ruin the organizations of a great king, the orders of an army commander or the practices of an influential person in history.

> *The Lord foils the plans of the nations; he thwarts the purposes of the peoples. But the plans of the Lord stand firm forever, the purposes of his heart through all generations.*
>
> (Psalms 33:10-11, NIV)

During the time of Deborah, when the Israelites began to rise up against the Canaanite oppression, the Canaanite king and his commanders probably had a grandiose plan for Israel's crushing defeat and further subjugation. It was likely a cruel plan to be executed by Sisera, the general of the Canaanite army. In this plan, there would be no peaceful co-existence, no freedom for the Israelites, no self-governance for the Israelites. In fact, it was undoubtedly Canaanite king Jabin's intent to keep the Israelites under his control for all time.

But God had other plans.

We see that God raised up Deborah at just the right time. Deborah was a prophetess and a powerful leader who commanded respect because of her faithfulness and trust in the Lord. She was responsible for bringing the people of Israel back to God. That was probably why Barak had wanted her to go with him. We don't read about blatant sin in her life—unlike Paul who killed Christians, Abraham who repeatedly lied, or many other Biblical leaders. This does not mean that she didn't have her weaknesses. But it is encouraging to me that the Bible depicts Deborah as a strong woman who eventually took the lead when the time came to take a stand for God.

For some unknown reason, God also picked Jael, a woman who was a relatively unknown tent-dweller, to kill the most powerful man on the battlefield. This amazing story is recorded in Judges 4:17-22. God delivered General Sisera into her hands. She gave him some warm milk and tucked him in under the covers. We do not know why she decided to kill Sisera, especially since her husband's clan had friendly relations with King Jabin. Who would have guessed that a woman like her would perform such a heroic act and be praised by both Deborah and Barak as the most blessed of women? (Judges 5:24) During a time when society did not respect or revere women as much as men, the Israelites sang her praises and described her actions in song. In light of Deborah's leadership and Barak's role, isn't it interesting that God ended up using Jael, a woman unfamiliar with the ways of war, to deliver the death blow to Sisera (Judges 4:9)?

The lesson is that God could have easily gotten rid of the Canaanites even without the aid of Deborah, Barak or Jael. And as we see in the case of Barak's fearful reluctance, God loved his people so much that he was going to answer their plea for help even if they sometimes fell short of his desire to use them.

Ultimately, God's plans have nothing to do with man's strategy or careful preparation. God has *his* plans and works through each one of us to fulfill his will for our lives and for those around us. We may be unbelievably talented and have wonderful ideas, but God may choose to work through someone different. We may be very capable, but God may call someone less capable to accomplish great things for society. We may have graduated at the top of the class, but God may decide to bless someone less educated to become a multi-millionaire.

I was watching a TV show on multi-millionaires who had won their fortunes by simply playing the lottery. These particular millionaires had won substantial amounts ranging anywhere from $70-100 million! These instant winners did not have Harvard or Yale degrees. Some of them had not even graduated from high school, but they were now enjoying a higher standard of living than many others who had slaved year after year to get advanced degrees so that they could have more lucrative careers. Obviously, planning and effort are very important, but that alone does not necessarily determine the specific outcome of our lives. Only God can do that.

God's ultimate intent was to save the Israelites, not to lift up Barak or anyone else as a hero. The Israelites were his people. He loved them. He chose them out of all the nations (Deuteronomy 7:8). In the same way, God wants to save us all today (1 Timothy 2:3-4). He loves us and chose us to be his children. And like any loving parent with their children, our Father in heaven has great plans for our lives. Those plans, however, might not be a part of *our* plans. Moreover, we might stumble and fail along the way. But that does not mess up his purposes for our lives. Look at Jonah when he was called by God. He ran away, but God caught up to him and used him anyway. Consider Moses. He made the excuse that he was not good at speaking, but he ended up doing a lot of talking to Pharaoh—which was quite impressive when you think about the intimidating circumstances.

During the time of Deborah, each piece of the puzzle was important in carrying out God's purposes. Deborah led the way. Barak commanded the attack. Jael single-handedly killed their enemy's leader. Moreover, the different tribes of Israel joined in the battle. Barak initially took ten thousand men as God commanded him, but others united with them to conquer the Canaanites, giving them peace for forty years after their victory (Judges 5:31). Definitively, we can see that no one was more important than the other. Each played a crucial role in conquering the Canaanites.

But I'm Not Good Enough

As women, we can sometimes feel insignificant, small or even worthless. Negative perceptions from our backgrounds and our upbringing can influence our thinking. We believe that God would never want to use someone like us for anything of great impact or of huge importance. We look at ourselves and see nothing but defects, blemishes and flaws. We're too fat. We're not smart enough. We're not as talented as we want to be. We're not attractive enough. For almost every calling, there seems to be a reason why we can't, why we're not ready, or why we're the wrong choice. As a result, we are frozen in place, immobile and unused. Sadly, we can end up making our fears of inadequacy and insignificance become a reality.

I believe that one of Satan's greatest lies to women is to convince us that we are useless, without value or inadequate. Often, all it takes is an insensitive comment made by someone we respect to throw us into a tailspin of negative thinking. We never consider that we might have misunderstood that person, or that we might have taken the comment the wrong way. Instead, we hear the words over and over again in our minds, and *we interpret them negatively,* making things worse. All our fears and insecurities then get validated. These destructive thoughts about ourselves bring in bitterness and hopelessness. They become absolute and destructive facts: *"I'm no good." "I could never do that." "No one believes in me."*

We can be so good at assuming the worst. Of course, along life's path, difficult times do occur. Unfortunately, if we are already expecting the worst, those experiences end up confirming our judgments and so we continue to imagine the most horrible scenarios almost every time. And yet, we must realize that those fears are based on our negative thoughts, not on the truth of what God is actually doing in our lives.

A few years ago, I was at a Christian conference where the theme was having a deeper faith in God. At the same location, there was another conference taking place about positive thinking. The main speaker for that conference was a famous and powerful lecturer. At the end of their conference, he had everyone convinced they could do anything if they would just believe. His crew set up hot burning coals across ten parking spaces in the hotel parking lot outside, and he asked all the attendees to walk barefoot on the coals one after another. I watched from my hotel room window as the mass of people lined up, about 200 in all, and each of them walked over the burning coals without burning themselves.

In the morning, I decided to introduce myself to one of the attendees from that other conference. I asked him if he had walked on the coals the night before. He said, "Yes." Then I inquired about how he was able to walk on burning coals without burning himself. He replied, "It was the coolest thing! The coals didn't even feel hot. I just believed that I could do anything, and it happened just as I believed. I'm fired up about going back and making tons of money for my business. Now, I know that I can really do it!"

The testimonials from that conference were the same from every person whether man or woman. As I passed them in the hallway, I initiated conversation, hoping to share my faith with them. Instead, I was convicted at my own lack of faith. It became embarrassing to me that these people believed more about making money and being successful than I believed in God's power. I witnessed the power of positive thinking without God. These people had not opened up a single scripture in the Bible throughout the whole weekend and yet were able to walk on burning coals with their bare feet! I realized that with God and his powerful word, I could undoubtedly do much greater things. With faith and positive *spiritual* thinking, God could accomplish so much more through little insignificant me.

We waste so much time on negative thinking. We get depressed. We get down on ourselves. Instead of expending all our valuable energy on what we can't do, wouldn't it be more worth our time to focus on what we *can* do? Starting from tiny ripples, even our small attempts can eventually become a tidal wave of impact. If we are willing to be led by God, then *he* can accomplish great things through our lives.

Through her life, Deborah showed the people of Israel what could happen when we believe that God is in control. She was not power hungry nor was she trying to take control over the Israelites single-handedly. In fact, she wanted the princes of Israel to take the lead. *On that day Deborah and Barak son of Abinoam sang this song: "When the princes in Israel take the lead, when the people willingly offer themselves— praise the LORD!"* (Judges 5:1-2, NIV)

Negative thinking affects people in the world just as much as it does God's people. When we dive into the cesspool of denial and doubt, we constrain and limit God's power in us. If people without the Holy Spirit can use positive thinking to impact their lives, imagine how much more we can do with God's true Spirit living inside of us.

It is vital for us to remember that God's amazing grace is such that we don't have to be perfect to be used by him. His Son died on the cross for us because God already knew that we are full of flaws, defects and blemishes. He knew who we really were, and he gave us the greatest gift possible—his forgiveness. We should also feel confident that still knowing us, he desires to give us the grace of using our lives to accomplish his significant purpose and will.

In God's kingdom, the cup is always half full and never half empty.
In God's family, all of his people are sinners—imperfect to the core—but are worth sacrificing for.
In God's heart, each soul is the apple of his eye (Zechariah 2:8).
In God's eyes, no one is worthless, because each soul has the same worth as Jesus' life.
In God's assessment, everyone is "good enough," because he created us as we are (Psalms 139:13-14).
In God's thoughts, anyone can do amazing things through him, even greater things than Christ. (John 14:12)

Consider this: Maybe, just maybe, in all of God's wisdom, he made us imperfect for one reason—to glorify himself. We were never meant to get the glory in the first place. And perhaps those glaring weaknesses in us are perfect for the plans he has for us. If we are insecure, disorganized, or fearful, perhaps it was supposed to be that way. Or if we are innately perfectionists or procrastinators, is it possible that we were meant to be that way? Maybe, in using imperfect people like us, God always intended to show his glory so that no one would be able to say, "*I* did it!" But, rather, God would be able to proclaim to the whole world, "Yes. It was me. I am your God and I did it all! Do you believe in me now? Are you convinced of my greatness?"

Prayerfully, when God shows his mercy and performs great miracles in our lives, all the people will say, "Amen. There is truly a God!" And Satan can never deceive us again with his empty words that convince us of our worthlessness, because everything we are, warts and all, is a part of God's plan. Therefore, as long as we are fine with God getting the credit for all the good that we do in our lives, we don't ever have to struggle with whether we are good enough or not, because God is good enough. God is amazing. God is in control. God is the one who works. And God should always be praised through Jesus Christ.

> *God can do anything, you know—far more than you could ever imagine or guess or request in your wildest dreams! He does it not by pushing us around but by working within us, his Spirit deeply and gently within us. Glory to God in the church! Glory to God in the Messiah, in Jesus! Glory down all the generations! Glory through all millennia! Oh, yes!*
> (Ephesians 3:20-21, The Message)

 ## QUESTIONS FOR THE HEART

1. Read Judges 4:4-8. When Deborah asks Barak to lead the charge against Jabin's army, Barak tells Deborah that he will not go unless Deborah was with him. Consider these two different personalities. Are you a natural leader like Deborah or are you someone who likes to follow like Barak? Whether or not you are a natural leader, have you ever been called to take leadership in your church? What was your response? Pray for God to lead you to have a godly response when you are called.

2. Who are the people in your life that you respect? What are the qualities in their life that draws you to them? Write down two or three characteristics that you would like to imitate in them.

3. God has a plan for each one of us. We are a part of an infinite tapestry of God's workings. How has God shown you *his* plans for your life? What was your attitude during the times when situations did not go according to your plans?

Chapter 6

RUTH AND NAOMI: FINDING LOVE THROUGH GRACE

Hope from Hopelessness

(Suggested Reading: Ruth 1 & 2)

I thoroughly enjoy love stories, especially the ones with happy endings where the woman or the man gets the person of his or her dreams. The book of Ruth is a love story—a story of deep devotion. It is also a book about God's grace through difficulties and obstacles in life. It shows God's faithfulness during a period in history when "everyone did as he saw fit" (Judges 17:6, 21:25). The Israelites lived in disobedience, idolatry and hostility. To many of the Israelites at the time, God seemed invisible and absent. They had drifted from their fervent love for him and exchanged their relationship with him for the worship of other gods.

Not Your Ordinary Love Story

This particular love story is not a conventional tale of love, but actually two stories knit into one. First, a mother-in-law named Naomi and a daughter-in-law, Ruth, demonstrate a deep and self-sacrificing devotion toward one another—a very unlikely pair with an extraordinary mutual commitment. The other story is how an older rich man, Boaz, and the same daughter-in-law fall in love. Their account begins with hopelessness and despair, but ends with God's hand working invisibly yet powerfully through the faithfulness of each of the main characters.

Our tale begins with Elimelech, an Israelite who leaves his people in Judah to escape a famine and to seek a better life. He chose to live among the pagans in Moab rather than with his own people in order to improve his chances for prosperity. Ironically, Elimelech died young and so did his sons, both of whom had married Moabite women. When we consider their lives, it seems that nothing turned out the way Elimelech had intended. Though his family had escaped the famine, they were also alienated from their heritage of faith. Though his sons married, neither produced an heir. Ultimately, Elimelech's compromises in his faith did not result in the blessings he had sought.

The scriptures have a very specific reference to the nation of Moab, Elimelech's adopted home:

> *No Ammonite or **Moabite** or any of his descendants may enter the assembly of the LORD, even down to the tenth generation. For they did not come to meet you with bread and water on your way when you came out of Egypt, and they hired Balaam son of Beor from Pethor in Aram Naharaim to pronounce a curse on you. However, the LORD your God would not listen to Balaam but turned the curse into a blessing for you, because the LORD your God loves you. **Do not seek a treaty of friendship with them as long as you live.***
>
> (Deuteronomy 23:3-6, NIV)

The Moabites were not allowed to enter into the assembly of the Lord down to the tenth generation. If God did not want his people to seek a treaty of friendship with the Moabites, imagine how he must have felt when Elimelech's sons, Mahlon and Kilion, married Moabite women.

Along the way, however, it is clear that Naomi never gave up her faith in the true God. She was a loyal wife who followed her husband and did her best despite challenging circumstances. She had built a great relationship with her daughters-in-law who were even willing to follow her back to her homeland. Naomi's attitude of faithfulness rubbed off especially on Ruth.

Unparalleled Devotion

After the deaths of their husbands, Naomi, Orpah and Ruth all were faced with a difficult decision for their future. In spite of her misfortune both of her daughters-in-law respected Naomi. In any other situation, Orpah and Ruth might have felt resentment toward their mother-in-law or have doubted in her god, as they watched Naomi experience tragedy upon tragedy, as well as being affected themselves. This could have produced cynicism in the God of Israel and hampered their faith. Instead, both women loved their mother-in-law deeply and sympathized with her as they suffered together.

In the midst of tragedy, Ruth maintained an amazing spirit of selflessness. When Naomi encouraged both her daughters-in-law to go back to their own people, the other daughter-in-law, Orpah, returned to Moab, but Ruth pleaded to be able to follow Naomi wherever she went. She must have been a very special person to instill Ruth not only with faith, but also with an unwavering faithfulness to her. Ruth's devotion to Naomi was truly self-sacrificing and extraordinary.

The dialogue between Ruth and Naomi shows how much God was a part of their relationship. We can assume that in the midst of a spiritually challenging situation in Moab, Naomi had done her best to convert her daughters-in-law to the Jewish ways. In return, God was gracious to this faithful widow and provided her with a special friend in Ruth. At a time when Naomi had no relatives in Moab, no source of income, no inheritance to support her and no chance to remarry, her daughter-in-law pledged to take care of her and to accompany her wherever she went.

Ruth made one of the most compelling vows recorded in the Bible. The depth of her vow was such that she gave her whole life and soul to her mother-in-law even though there was no promise of a better future by staying with her. To this day, Ruth's touching words are used in many wedding vows:

> *But Ruth replied, "Don't urge me to leave you or to turn back from you. Where you go I will go, and where you stay I will stay. Your people will be my people and your God my God. Where you die I will die, and there*

I will be buried. May the LORD deal with me, be it ever so severely, if anything but death separates you and me."

(Ruth 1:16-17, NIV)

It can be said that at this moment, Ruth became a true Jew by accepting the God of Israel with no conditions attached. Her life was given over to Naomi's people and to her God. She gave an oath, which she kept throughout the rest of her life. And God honors such an alien.

*"You are to distribute this land among yourselves according to the tribes of Israel. You are to allot it as an inheritance for yourselves and for the **aliens** who have settled among you and who have children. You are to consider them as native-born Israelites; along with you they are to be allotted an inheritance among the tribes of Israel. In whatever tribe the **alien** settles, there you are to give him his inheritance," declares the Sovereign LORD.*

(Ezekiel 47:21-23, NIV)

Life can bring on so many unexpected tragedies and challenges. Naomi was a woman who followed her husband with a submissive heart, ready to do what was right. She may have not agreed with her husband's decision, but nonetheless followed him to their new life in Moab. Tragically, the result was witnessing the death of her husband and two sons, and being left with only her two daughters-in-law. Understandably, Naomi battled with the growing bitterness in her heart, and upon her return to Bethlehem, she told the people to no longer call her Naomi (meaning *pleasant*), but Mara (meaning *bitter*).

"...I went away full, but the Lord has brought me home empty. Why call me Naomi when the Lord has caused me to suffer and the Almighty has sent such tragedy upon me?"

(Ruth 1:19-21, NLT)

When Naomi returned home, the women of Bethlehem were excited to see her, but in Naomi's bitterness, she told everyone that she went away full but came back empty. But did she really return empty? She had returned to Bethlehem with a faithful and devoted daughter-in-law in Ruth. God showed her incredible grace despite her bitterness. He had answered one of Naomi's greatest prayers with Ruth converting to Judaism. She had not come back empty, but blessed with an answered prayer. She, however, could not see this because of her negative and dark mindset.

Answered prayers sometimes come at the most unexpected times. When we are going through the toughest of times, we might not recognize God's loving hand blessing us with one of our greatest desires. God was faithful to Naomi during her darkest times. She was struggling through her pain and had become bitter, but God kept working behind the scenes. In fact, Naomi experienced unparalleled devotion from both God and Ruth.

Relationships That Bring Grace

We women are connectors and empathizers. When we go through rough times, we need friends, sisters, mothers or daughters to stand beside us. We need others to understand us and to bond with us in order to get through the difficulties. We search for those relationships and yearn for them. Sometimes, husbands or boyfriends are simply not enough. Even friends whom we have known for years may not exactly meet our needs either. But during those moments of need, God can surprise us with acquaintances or other relatives who seem to have the right words and who have experienced similar pain.

God works in ways we do not totally understand. We question pain. We wonder why. We can become angry and bitter. But God is always gracious, showing us compassion and comfort, often in the form of a relationship. He provided Naomi with Ruth, a woman who did not judge her or abandon her. He also provided Ruth with an amazing mother-in-law who guided her with wisdom in the ways of the Lord. In the same way, God will provide when we are hurting. It may not be in the same way as he did for Ruth or Naomi. But we can be completely confident that God's quiet hand is at work.

An excited young bride, Mayo moved from Japan to the United States to marry my brother, Hiroshi. They had a baby and began a new life together, purchasing a house just outside New York City. However, just two years later, Hiroshi died in a tragic car accident at the age of thirty. My nephew, Hiroaki, was only a toddler at the time. Reeling from her sudden loss, my sister-in-law was confused and grieving. It was a complete shock for Mayo to lose her young husband.

Mayo was a stay-at-home mom with no profession while my brother worked as a financial consultant. She was a foreigner in the United States, now alone with her little boy. Since her family, her relatives and closest friends were all in Japan, she had no one to confide in during this traumatic time. Throughout the funeral and during the arrangement of my brother's affairs, she wrestled with what to do about her and her son's future.

Meanwhile, my husband and I were living in Tokyo, Japan. When we heard the news, we were in complete disbelief. We rushed back to New York to be with Mayo and Hiroaki. My personal devastation was deep, as my brother was my only sibling. Both my sister-in-law and I experienced deep loss and unbelievable grief. Even as I look back today, much of my memory of that time is just a blur with only flashes of images remaining. But one thing I remember is that I prayed very hard for God's guidance and, like a voice from heaven speaking to me, I felt God telling me to take in my sister-in-law and nephew into our home in Tokyo until she could get back on her feet again.

Though my intent for her living with us was for her benefit, I felt that God gave me a way to heal my broken heart. Mayo and I became the best of friends during the year she and Hiroaki lived with us. We were able to help one another during our hard days when the sadness was overwhelming. Some days would be harder for her and other days would be harder for me. In the midst of it all, through God's grace, Mayo became a Christian and gained great strength from the Lord.

As I write these words, tomorrow marks eighteen years since the death of my brother. Looking back, there have definitely been some difficult times. But I can also see so many victories and powerful ways that God worked to transform a hopeless situation into one that brings complete glory to him.

First of all, my sister-in-law is remarried to a wonderful Christian man named Rob Narita who used to perform on Broadway and is now on many TV shows as a professional actor. Secondly, together they now have two more lovely children—a daughter and a son. Thirdly, Hiroaki became a Christian. Could God have done any better than that?

I believe that this was all a result of Mayo's faith to move to Tokyo. Her own hometown in central Japan was just a several hour train ride away; yet she chose to come live with us. She had to overcome great odds being a single mother for a few years, but fought through by her faith in Christ. She remains a faithful Christian to this day, always giving her best to God. Mayo is an example of a modern day Ruth to me.

To this day, Mayo and I are very close. God has provided me with a wonderful sister. Praise God for bringing us from hopelessness to hope.

Finding Grace Through Bitter Times
(Suggested Reading: Ruth 3 & 4)

From what we can tell, neither Ruth nor Naomi did anything to merit a life of widowhood. Naomi herself may have wondered why her life was cursed and why God did not take her life along with her husband and two sons. As an older woman, it was nearly impossible for her to remarry and to start a new life.

But in spite of all her bitterness, Naomi made a decision that pleased God. She decided to go back to her people, back to the land of her God. Most likely, Naomi had never bonded closely with those who lived in Moab and yearned for her friendships and relatives back at home—to be with the friends she grew up with and with her relatives. In her pain and loneliness, she ached for those who could help her and guide her.

This decision, in turn, gave Ruth the courage to move to a city and to a people that was foreign to her. She moved to the land of the God to whom she had committed her life. In a situation such as Ruth's and Naomi's, we can either become immobilized or confounded by our fear of the future and the unknown. Other times, we can act out of sheer emotion leading us to make unwise decisions, which we may later regret. By choosing a path that would bring them closer to their God, both Ruth and Naomi were able to make a wise decision for their lives even if they couldn't specifically see all the future would bring. When we can't see the road ahead, and we don't know what to do, the one choice we can always make is to lean toward God. In that simple decision, there is wisdom.

When Grief Becomes Bitterness

In the spring of 1995, I traveled from Tokyo to New York to see the doctor who had been treating my lupus. I was staying with my brother, Hiroshi, and his wife, Mayo. On that trip, my doctor informed me that my disease was "officially" in remission, and I was able to share this jubilant news with both of them. Less than six months later, however, Hiroshi passed away and thus began a domino effect of tragedy for the following year of my life.

My grandmother, who had helped raised my brother and me, was deeply upset by the death of her grandson. She suffered from Parkinson's disease, and the news caused her illness take a turn for the worse. Within five months, my grandmother also passed away. A month after her death, I also experienced another miscarriage, probably linked to the immense sadness in my heart.

Though my sister-in-law became a Christian, Satan utilized my brother's death and these other sad events to rob the joy away from me. On the one hand, Mayo's life had radically changed and, as a result, Hiroaki also transformed into a joyful and loving little boy. Yet the grief in my heart ate up much of the happiness I should have felt, and it eventually became difficult to see anything positive in my life. I became convinced that I was living in a never-ending nightmare.

Grief after grief piled on so heavy that I could not sleep at night. I made myself busy and neglected to take care of my health. As a result, a backache that had been bothering me continually worsened until one night I bent down in the shower to pick up a bar of soap that I had dropped, only to cause something in my back to give out. I began to scream so loud that my husband thought that someone had broken into the house and was trying to hurt me. He found me curled up on the shower floor unable to move, crying and screaming as the water continued to pour onto me. An ambulance took me to the hospital where we were told that I had ruptured a disc in my lower back.

The pain from the ruptured disk was unlike any pain I had before, making childbirth seem almost easy in comparison. For a month, the doctors administered a morphine drip so that I could sleep at night. After two months of traction and heavy doses of painkillers, the doctors decided that I needed surgery. For the operation, my husband took me to the famous Mayo Clinic in Minnesota. The Mayo Clinic is near his hometown, and his parents were able to take care of me during the post-op recovery period that lasted several months.

During the painful months before my operation, two friends made some insensitive comments to me that were extremely hurtful. I'm sure they meant me no harm, and I wish that I could have been strong enough to handle their inadvertently wounding words, but something inside of me shattered. With all that I had gone through, I yearned for sympathy and compassion but received the exact opposite. One of my friends took my moment of weakness as an opportunity to tell me how God was trying to teach me a lesson. And my other friend was not even thinking about what I was going through. Instead, she criticized me for the ways I had not met her personal needs. I felt kicked when I was down. As a result, I became very bitter and angry.

> *"Don't call me Naomi," she told them. "Call me Mara, because the Almighty has made my life very bitter. I went away full, but the Lord has brought me back empty. Why call me Naomi? The Lord has afflicted me; the Almighty has brought misfortune upon me."*
>
> (Ruth 1:20-21, NIV)

These are the words that Naomi spoke after experiencing intense grief. We all endure sorrow, wounds and death. Sometimes those sorrows can leave scars in our hearts and make us bitter. We blame God and others, not knowing how to heal the pain that continues to grip us through life.

In the same way, deep bitterness took root inside of me and began to consume my life. It affected my marriage and my ability to help the women in my church. I saw through negative and soot-covered glasses in every situation. Even though my husband tried hard to love me through that time, my heart was unyielding to the anger and resentments that bubbled over in my heart. Eventually, however, I realized that I needed comfort and knew that I could not resolve the confusion and pain on my own.

Grace That Listens

I finally asked Frank if I could go back to the states and get help from two dear friends who had known me for many years. My husband called my friends, but they insisted on flying out to be with me in Tokyo during my time of grief. I was so happy and grateful that they would make the effort to be with me. After they both arrived, we went away to a little bed and breakfast inn outside of Tokyo to spend three days together. During my time with them, I cried, wept and poured out my heart. They never judged me or criticized me even as I gushed out my bitter thoughts. Afterward, I felt a hundred pounds lighter having confessed the hurt and the bitterness in my heart toward people and God.

Bitterness and unforgiveness are Satan's great tools to keep us far away from God. When we go through "bitter" times—times that make us vulnerable to Satan's schemes, we are more susceptible to being offended by people, to getting our feelings hurt and to questioning God's goodness. In the name of trying to encourage us, well-meaning people may quote scriptures about trusting God and about learning a lesson through our woes and misery, but their words sometimes seem to embitter us even more. These words were never meant to hurt us, but we hear them differently when we are going through tough times. Those same scriptures and thoughts may have even encouraged us in the past, but we hear them differently now that we are going through extremely tough times. When a friend or loved one is going through moments like these, often the greatest gift that we can give is to simply listen with grace.

I remember a couple of other friends in Tokyo who simply hugged me and sat next to me not saying a word. Their presence gave me the greatest strength. After they had been with me in silence for an hour, I tried to send them home, thinking they had many other things to do. But they insisted on staying with me for several more hours. I was so comforted by them. I kept offering them food and drink, but they were adamant about my doing nothing for them. They apologized that they had nothing to say and felt inadequate to help me. But their devotion and humility consoled me more than any platitudes or correct words ever could.

Extraordinary Surrender

Ruth never gave up trying to take care of her mother-in-law. She was a young widow trying to console an older woman who had lost her husband and two sons. Ruth insisted on staying with Naomi even though she herself mourned the loss of her husband—an incredibly selfless act of love during the most painful time in her life. It is much like the love of Jesus, who while hanging on the cross, looked at his disciple John and asked him to take care of his mother.

When Jesus then saw His mother, and the disciple whom He loved standing nearby, He said to His mother, "Woman, behold, your son!" Then He said to the disciple, "Behold, your mother!" From that hour the disciple took her into his own household.

(Matthew 19:26-28, NASB)

This type of extraordinary love is extremely rare. Most people in extreme pain can only focus on themselves. Anguish, torment and distress are not ingredients that encourage us to give to others. Sacrificial acts come at a time when we are strong and able, not when we are defenseless and insecure. Yet, this is what our Savior did for us. We will never know the physical, emotional and spiritual trauma that our Lord experienced on the cross. But it was at the cross that Jesus showed his greatest love, his perfect devotion and complete submission to God— for our sake, he drank from the cup of suffering with a willing heart (Matthew 26:39-44). Through Christ's example, we can learn to have the same attitude.

This is the kind of life you've been invited into, the kind of life Christ lived. He suffered everything that came his way so you would know that it could be done, and also know how to do it, step-by-step. He never did one thing wrong, Not once said anything amiss. They called him every name in the book and he said nothing back. He suffered in silence, content to let God set things right. He used his servant body to carry our sins to the Cross so we could be rid of sin, free to live the right way. His wounds became your healing.

(1 Peter 1:23-24, The Message)

The Message spells it out in harsh reality: As followers of Jesus we have been invited to this "kind of life"—a life with suffering. Jesus did nothing wrong. He didn't even sin one time. Yet people taunted him, ridiculed him and killed him. He suffered in silence and continued to give of himself to the very end knowing that God would set things right. Jesus' extraordinary love for each one of us was reflected in his willingness to surrender himself.

Perhaps one of the highest forms of love is learning how to forgive. Forgiveness is a choice. It does not necessarily mean that we completely trust or become best friends with the people who have hurt us, especially in extreme cases like abuse. However, it is a clear decision to no longer allow bitterness to control our lives. Our natural tendency is to desire retribution or, at least, insist on fervent apologies before releasing a person from the prison we have created for them in our minds. I believe that forgiveness is an act of surrender in which we take the power of revenge out of our own hands and give it over to God. Obviously, if we can restore the relationship to where it used to be, it can be a true victory in Christ. However, the one who sins against us can never take away what they did.

I found it interesting that in the Japanese Bible, the *kanji* (a Japanese written alphabet) word for forgiveness contains the character for the color red—seemingly symbolizing blood and the cross. True forgiveness comes at the cost of the forgiver and is free to the person who is forgiven. And yet, if we withhold our forgiveness, the cost is so much higher and devastating. When we refuse to forgive or to let go of the bitterness we have, it hurts *our* hearts and *our* relationship with God. The person who hurt us may never know how we feel and may be living in complete ignorance of our bitterness. In the meantime, our souls continue to be devoured by raging emotions that keep us under Satan's power.

Many times, because of our lack of forgiveness, there is so much pain in us that we end up punishing those we love and not the actual offenders. We can target our husbands, our parents and our children when the wrongdoer was none of these people. We unrealistically expect these people to somehow take away our pain when only God can truly heal the wounds in our hearts. I know that I did this to my husband after my mother's death. As I shared in an earlier chapter, I struggled with bitterness toward my father, and even toward my mother for having abandoned me. My husband tried his best to console me, but I wanted him to take away my pain, which was an impossible expectation. When he could not help me as I desired, I became angry and frustrated. Over time, I had to learn that only God was able to deeply heal my wound. He led me to experience empathy and forgiveness toward my parents. I had to decide to truly trust in God and not to put it on others to "fix" me and to "help" me.

Naomi honestly acknowledged the bitterness that had taken root in her heart. But she didn't let it destroy her life. Both Ruth and Naomi surrendered their hearts to the God of Israel, leaving behind their pain as they made their way back to Bethlehem. Each of them chose the same path as Jesus and helped one another overcome bitter times through selfless service. They leaned on one another and allowed their friendship and loyalty to each other to sustain them through the difficulties.

I often think of how our godly decisions, in the midst of our weaknesses, can be the avenue through which God can truly glorify himself. God knows that we are weak beings who need his guidance and direction. But only we can choose to surrender our lives to him. Paradoxically, it is when we raise up our arms in surrender that God raises us up in victory, because he can truly take over. When we relinquish all our human control, all authority transfers to God—the one who knows so much better than ourselves.

Grace Heals Our Wounds

Recently, I was listening to the radio and heard about a product that takes all stretch marks and old scars away. All you had to do was to apply this cream on your stretch marks for thirty days, and they were supposed to disappear. The product came with a thirty-day money back guarantee. Of course, after having three babies, my body was left with some battle scars as some of you other ladies out there can relate to. So I called into the radio station and ordered this "miracle" scar remover. After thirty days, there was minimal progress, so I got the second bottle to apply it for thirty *more* days. (They really had me hooked.) Well, you can imagine what happened next. My crusade to get rid of my marks did not work. There was no money back, because I purchased the second cream. The guarantee was only for the first bottle, which I already used up! So I was left with the same old body and less money in the bank.

Many of us do the same thing with the wounds in our hearts. We put band-aids on our hurts and even on our bitterness, hoping that ignoring them will make them go away. We cover them up with a tough façade, so that no one will touch our tender spots. We put on "miracle" creams, which are lies from Satan convincing us that we are justified to live with resentments because of what others have done to us. And all the while, the damage remains, never healing, never fading but continuing to erode our faith.

Did you know that once we have a physical scar from an injury, the healed skin on it is tougher than the unharmed skin around it? God made our bodies so that wounds would be healed by skin that is stronger, so that it is more difficult to injure that same exact spot again. In the same way, once we heal from the wounds in our hearts, we will be more equipped to handle greater difficulties in the same area.

A scripture in the book of Peter says that by Christ's wounds, we are healed (1 Peter 2:24). What does that mean? Jesus subjected himself to punishment and death so that we don't have to live in our sins any longer, nor do we have to be controlled by the sins of others. When God freed us, he gave us the power to give grace to others as well. He forgave us, so that we no longer have to live in hostility or anger. God took away every sin—even the ones we didn't know we had. At the same time, this conviction is not as easy and clean as we would want it to be. In fact, it can be a rather painful process. It would be so nice if we could just snap a finger and all the hurts and wounds would just disappear. And we could live happily ever after.

But this is Satan's world. And he doesn't work that way. He wants to keep those wounds planted deep inside of us, never intending for us to let go of them. He will keep poking at the same spot so that it will never heal. Honestly, there is no easy answer to resolve our emotions, but the Bible gives us a solution that goes against our rationale and against the grain of society. It is found in the scripture, which says that it is more "blessed to give than to receive" (Acts 20:35). Blessed means *superlatively happy.* Yet, the world tells us that when we get what we *want*, we are happy—not when we *give*.

After my surgery and four months of rehab, I was able to return to my "normal" life. Though my body was healing, I realized that my spirit was still damaged, because I no longer had a brother, mother and grandmother to give me security and to take care of me during the tough times as well as someone to rejoice with me during the happy times. On top of that, during that same year, I didn't get the baby that I had been praying over many years, but ended up losing two more. I had put band-aids and "miracle" cream on. None of those false solutions were working for me. I tried to push away my feelings, but found myself unhappy and unsettled. I became a time bomb. All it would take was another sad event or tragedy to push me over the edge.

Naomi pushed through her sorrow and grief to take care of Ruth. God saw Naomi's mindset and blessed her efforts with success.

> *One day Naomi her mother-in-law said to her, "My daughter, should I not try to find a home for you, where you will be well provided for? Is not Boaz, with whose servant girls you have been, a kinsman of ours? Tonight he will be winnowing barley on the threshing floor. Wash and perfume yourself, and put on your best clothes. Then go down to the threshing floor, but don't let him know you are there until he has finished eating and drinking.*

(Ruth 3:1-3, NIV)

Naomi decided that it was time for Ruth to stop mourning and to stop living for her mother-in-law. It was time for Ruth to move on in her life and to start a new life with another spouse. For Naomi to make such a decision for Ruth was a big step of faith. Naomi and Ruth were not related by blood, so she may have worried that Ruth would abandon her and cleave to her new mate. Naomi, however, took a chance and encouraged Ruth to initiate a relationship with a kinsman from her husband's family.

Ruth's faith and trust were also put to the test when her mother-in-law asked her to put herself in a vulnerable position, one that could have been met with hurtful rejection. Naomi's instructions to Ruth were pretty forward for a woman of that time. Ruth might have been taken aback and thought: *Wash myself, put perfume on, put on my best clothes? Then sleep at the man's feet? And do whatever he tells me to do after that? What if it doesn't work out? Maybe I'm not ready to remarry. Besides, the guy might reject me because I'm not an Israelite.*

Ruth was a foreigner in a foreign land. She might have been plagued with doubts about how she would be accepted in this new society. Yet, Ruth obeyed her mother-in-law and followed her instructions. She overcame any insecurity or fear that she might have had and leaned on the wisdom and guidance of her mother-in-law. The result was that God's grace worked powerfully in Boaz's heart as he was touched by her initiative, calling her a woman of noble character (Ruth 3:11).

After experiencing so much tragedy as well as illness, I began to have a softer heart toward those who were hurting. I especially felt a need to help the older women in our church who were also experiencing health issues and tragedies of their own. For this reason, I decided to begin a "mom's" ministry, which was a Bible study group for older women. We started with a potluck lunch then a lesson. The small group of twenty women grew to over a hundred women each week! We eventually had to divide up into smaller groups to meet all the needs.

Many of those wonderful women "adopted" me as their daughter and took care of me even through some of the challenges that Satan would later put in my path. They were an incredible source of support to me, both personally and in our ministry in Japan. They possessed so much wisdom and insight from having lived a much longer life. I was blessed, more than that, I was superlatively happy as I tried to serve these women. In fact, they ended up fulfilling a greater need in me than I was ever able to provide for them. I saw through this time, that by the grace of giving, I received immense healing.

The Grace of God's Plans

In the inspiring story of Ruth, we can see God's amazing grace in the way he had set the stage for Boaz and Ruth's relationship. Unlike most of his countrymen, Boaz was open to taking a foreign widow as his wife. Why?

Well, you see, Boaz's mother was Rahab.

Yes, that Rahab. The prostitute—and the foreigner. Perhaps there was a stigma against Boaz because of his lineage, explaining why a rich man like himself was still an eligible bachelor at an older age. Boaz himself said he was surprised that Ruth did not go running after the younger men (Ruth 3:10). God also showed his mercy when Boaz stepped forward as a kinsman redeemer to Naomi's husband. Was this simply a coincidence or God's hand at work? Of course, this was God's kind favor toward an alien who wanted to worship him. Out of all the men of the town, God had placed Boaz in Ruth's path in the right place and at the right time. Could God have done a finer job of setting the scene for his wonderful plan?

*Salmon was the father of **Boaz (whose mother was Rahab).***
Boaz was the father of Obed (whose mother was Ruth).

Obed was the father of Jesse.
Jesse was the father of King David.
David was the father of Solomon (whose mother was Bathsheba, the widow of Uriah).

(Matthew 1:5-6, NLT)

Looking at the scripture above reveals God's incredible plan with startling clarity. God put two foreigners and a prostitute in the lineage of our savior, Jesus Christ, to display his infinite grace. At a time in society when people looked down on the prostitutes, the foreigners and the widows, God showed his immeasurable and eternal compassion. Even today, so many societies would shun someone from a disrespectable background like prostitution. Imagine allowing your son to marry a former prostitute. At a time in society when people looked down on the prostitutes, the foreigners and the widows, God showed his immeasurable compassion toward those whom many would consider among the weakest or most sinful by including them in the most glorious part of his eternal plan.

In the end, God worked powerfully through Naomi and Ruth. They were blessed because of their faithfulness to the Lord. The scriptures say that God not only restored Naomi's life, but sustained her in her old age.

So Boaz took Ruth, and she became his wife, and he went in to her. And the LORD enabled her to conceive, and she gave birth to a son. Then the women said to Naomi, "Blessed is the LORD who has not left you without a redeemer today, and may his name become famous in Israel." May he also be to you a restorer of life and a sustainer of your old age; for your daughter-in-law, who loves you and is better to you than seven sons, has given birth to him." Then Naomi took the child and laid him in her lap, and became his nurse. The neighbor women gave him a name, saying, "A son has been born to Naomi!" So they named him Obed. He is the father of Jesse, the father of David.

(Ruth 4:11-17, NASB)

God enabled Ruth to have a child after being with Boaz. Though Ruth had been initially married for about ten years (Ruth 1:4), Naomi had not been able to experience the joy of being a grandmother. Through her grandchild, Obed, Naomi was given a future full of joyful expectation. She went from a life of hopelessness to a life sustained by God's faithfulness. According to her neighbors, God had blessed Naomi with a daughter-in-law who was better than seven sons, and a child considered her own flesh and blood. She was no longer bitter *Mara*, but *Naomi*, which means pleasant and delightful.

God showed his grace in having a plan for a prostitute then later a foreigner and a bitter woman. He wanted them to be in the lineage of his own son. What an incredible and loving God we have!

 QUESTIONS FOR THE HEART

1. Read Ruth 1:6-22. Look at Naomi's attitude in the midst of hardship. Look at Ruth and her devotion to her mother-in-law. What characteristics would you want to imitate from each of them? When you look at Naomi and Ruth's lives, who do you identify with more? What decisions will you make based on the outcome of their lives?

2. Who is the modern-day "Naomi" or "Ruth" to you? What qualities in that woman exemplify a life of faith? The next time you see that person, ask her specifically how she overcame through her struggles. Also, make sure that she knows how much she is an inspiration to you so that she will continue strong in her faith.

3. We all have wounds in our hearts from life. Some of those wounds have left bitter feelings inside.

"For he wounds, but he also binds up; he injures, but his hands also heal."

Job 5:18.

Meditate on this scripture today as you think about the wounds in your heart.

Chapter 7

HANNAH: FINDING SELF-WORTH THROUGH GRACE

Finding True Self-Worth

(Suggested Reading: 1 Samuel 1 & 2:1-11)

All of us at one point or another will experience being victimized by someone else's malice or abuse. Whether it occurs one time or in a series of events—bullying hurts. Many times, the pain is especially deep because those who are supposedly close to us like friends or even family instigate the insensitive statements or abusive actions. Sadly, memories of such harsh treatment stay with us for years, working their way deep inside our hearts as they destroy our self-worth. Perhaps we've been teased about a personality quirk or some physical aspect like a stutter or birth defect. Or, we may have some kind of emotional or mental disability that has attracted the ignorant scorn of others. Being a target of such insults can have a lasting impact, dismantling our self-confidence.

On a similar note, many of us have experienced criticism and taunts about our faith in God and his word. Unfortunately, this seems to be a growing trend in our increasingly secularized society. Even centuries ago, our Lord knew that this would happen, and he encouraged us to rejoice (Matthew 5:10-12). It's a clear command, but it doesn't always take away the sting that such opposition can bring.

Hannah was a woman living during the time of the judges of Israel. Because she was barren, Peninnah, the other wife of her husband, would provoke her.

> *So Peninnah would taunt Hannah and make fun of her because the Lord had kept her from having children. Year after year it was the same—Peninnah would taunt Hannah as they went to the Tabernacle. Each time, Hannah would be reduced to tears and would not even eat.*
>
> (1 Samuel 1:6-7, NLT)

Peninnah abused Hannah by her heartlessness. This continued for years, reducing Hannah to tears and making her lose her appetite. Peninnah was merciless in her onslaught, as she persisted in hurting Hannah. It was over an issue that Hannah could not alter. She did not have the power within herself to address the matter as only God could decide whether or not to give her children.

As reflected in this short passage, I'm sure each of us can relate in some way to the pain that Hannah must have felt for many years. In those days, so much of the societal purpose of women was to bear children and produce a male heir. It was a measure of a woman's worth in society. So, in effect, Hannah had two hurdles to overcome—her sense of purpose not being fulfilled—and problems with Peninnah who she could not escape as she was "married" to her through Elkanah. As a result, in her desperation she turned to God.

Hannah went up to the Lord's house and prayed with all her strength. It was such a fervent and emotional prayer that Eli, the priest, mistook her entreaty to God as the ravings of a drunken woman who was out of control. He even confronted her during her prayer time (1 Samuel 1:13-14). Hannah, however, did not get angry or defensive but told Eli how deeply troubled she was. He then blessed her prayers, and she was able to go away with peace in her heart (1 Samuel 1:17-18).

Hannah had every reason to grow angry and bitter in her faith. The priest had even initially misunderstood her. Yet, as defective as she might have felt for not having children, she had a wonderful way about her that made Elkanah love her more than Peninnah. Peninnah was probably jealous and wanted to focus on Hannah's one fault—her inability to bear children. But instead of focusing on her barrenness and allowing it to make her feel worthless, Hannah focused on God. She overcame the critical words of Peninnah by putting her hope and trust in her Lord.

Grace Gives Us Significance

We ladies are all "barren" in one way or another. We can feel defective and worthless, or we may have people in our lives who provoke us to feel inadequate. Those times can elicit anger, frustration, bitterness and, for some of us, a desire to fight back. The reality is that all of us have an issue in our lives over which we have no control. It is up to God to make those changes and not up to us to alter them.

One thing that I have learned after nearly thirty years of counseling is that people often become mean when they are unhappy about something within themselves. They envy others who seem to have more, and make it their quest to make sure "happy" people become as unhappy as they are. They make biting comments and gossip about those who are cheery, to bring them down. God does not want us to be overcome by those unhappy people. He wants us to look to him and get our confidence and self-worth from him.

There is not a person on this earth who has not had some dysfunctional aspects in their life. As a child, you might have experienced abuse. At work, you might have been treated unfairly. At school, you might have been picked on during your early years. You might have excelled in sports but could never figure out the simplest math problems. You might have been an incredible student but were never able to throw the ball straight. You might have had children, but you could not connect well with them through the years.

I was the classic nerd in middle and high school. I was math club president, math team captain, top science award winner, computer club member, and top honor roll. And, yes, I wore glasses—and being Asian didn't help the stereotype of how people viewed me. I didn't like looking in the mirror, because I believed that I was ugly. In fact, looking in the mirror would steal away what little confidence I had in myself, so I would avoid them altogether. I had friends who were athletic and popular, mostly because they needed help from me with their math or science assignments. While they all played their sports after school or went out on dates on the weekends, I was tutoring other students. At times, I would be teased for being the teacher's pet or class nerd. On top of all of this, of course, I was always one of the last ones picked, if not the last one, during PE class when we divided up into teams. I was known as the cute little "Chinese" girl (even though I'm Japanese) nicknamed "Shinbones," because I was so skinny. On top of all of this, I was so shy, that my peers often overlooked my presence.

One time, a gang of kids from school beat up my brother and me because of racial prejudice. It happened outside of school, so one of my friends reported it to two policemen in a cruiser right in the vicinity as we were getting beaten up. The policemen just laughed at my friend as she tried to get help. Later, her mother took us to the police station, and she reported the officers who refused to help us. Those officers lied and said that they "checked it out," but saw nothing. Sometimes, because of who we are and for nothing we have done, we can be treated unfairly and rudely.

Later, those same bullies felt guilty after what happened. And since I didn't say anything about them at school, they tried extremely hard to be nice for the rest of the year to my brother and me. Nonetheless, that painful event taught me to never have prejudices against anyone, because it was such a painful experience. I do not ever wish to make anyone feel "less" by my attitude, actions or words because of their race or background.

For many years I grew up thinking I was insignificant and unimportant. Then I remember one night getting down on my knees, before I became a Christian, and prayed to God that it would be all right if I never became beautiful or popular, but that God would allow me to someday make a difference in people's lives. After I prayed that prayer, I felt at peace believing that I could become someone who impacted others and that it wouldn't matter how I looked or how many friends I had.

Just three short years later, God called me into his wonderful kingdom through an invitation to a Bible study group on campus during my freshman year at Tufts University. I became friends with Lynne, the group leader. After a series of Bible studies, Lynne helped me to understand God's plan for my life, and I eventually decided to become a Christian. Now, I look back on the past thirty years of my life and laugh at how God used an insignificant nerd like me in many cities on different continents to impact women for Jesus. It is clearly through the grace of God and his power that I have been able to find my self-worth and the confidence to influence others.

In the Old Testament, when Jeremiah was first called to be a prophet, he tried to tell God that he was too young and unable to speak on behalf of God. He only saw the imperfections in himself. He thought he was not capable of completing the task. But God encouraged him and reassured him that his presence would be with him so he would be safeguarded and made able. In this way, God's power could be clearly seen through his life.

> *The Lord gave me this message:*
>
> *"I knew you before I formed you in your mother's womb.*
>
> *Before you were born I set you apart and appointed you as my prophet to the nations."*
>
> *"O Sovereign Lord," I said, "I can't speak for you! I'm too young!"*
>
> *The Lord replied, "Don't say, 'I'm too young,' for you must go wherever I send you and say whatever I tell you. And don't be afraid of the people, for I will be with you and will protect you. I, the Lord, have spoken!"*
>
> (Jeremiah 1:4-8, NLT)

Some of us will be like Jeremiah who made excuses and told God he had made a mistake by choosing him. We should note that God did not suddenly make Jeremiah older or more competent as a result of his prayers and his rationalizations. In God's great wisdom and judgment, Jeremiah was created for the commission before him. God knew what he was doing. In the same way, we were made a certain way to fulfill a plan that he has for our lives (Psalms 139:13-16).

I never became an Olympic star or the captain of a sports team. But I did become an athlete for God—a runner who is running the race to heaven. (1 Corinthians 9:24) Like Hannah, some of us may be told, "Yes," much later in life and receive a long sought blessing. If so, it is important to rejoice in the wonderful gift and rest assured in God's timing. On the other hand, some of us may remain "barren" in a specific area of our lives no matter how long we wait. Either way, our faith should be based on the conviction that whatever our limitations may be, God will use them to glorify his name. In admitting our weaknesses, we affirm God's power within us, and we become better vessels for his purposes.

If there is a Peninnah (or several Peninnahs!) in your life, God knows how you feel. He looks at you differently than those critics do. You cannot allow the opinions of others to determine your self-worth. I believe I have wasted a lot of time in my life trying to get my confidence from what others say or think, when I have really needed to get it from God.

Over the years, I have learned to embrace my "barrenness" instead of fighting it. I have learned to accept who I am, not based on how others judge me, but based on the fact that I was important enough for Jesus to die for me. To him, I am significant. And he will use me if I continue to walk in his steps.

Have there been negative comments or biting criticisms that still cause you to doubt your value to God, or weaken your faith that God is using you? Whatever those wounding words are that keep echoing in your mind, you do not have to give them power over you any longer. You can be freed from the "Peninnahs" in your life.

Believe God more than those people. Acknowledge how God treats you and value that more than how those bullies regard you. By God's grace, you will indeed make a difference, because you were created to be significant in God's sight.

Allowing God's Grace to Heal Our Relationships

Relationships are central to our lives. For many of us, our relationships are our greatest source of joy—and paradoxically, our greatest source of heartache. Just because we are Christians doesn't mean that we have a free pass to avoid relationship conflicts. Even in the early church, men and women had difficulty in their relationships. In the church in Philippi, Euodia and Syntyche's relationship was so bad that Paul felt compelled to write about it in his letter to the Philippians so that the whole church could help them out:

I plead with Euodia and I plead with Syntyche to agree with each other in the Lord. Yes, and I ask you, loyal yokefellow, help these women who have contended at my side in the cause of the gospel, along with Clement and the rest of my fellow workers, whose names are in the book of life.

(Philippians 4:2-3, NIV)

Can you imagine being Euodia and Syntyche and hearing a letter like this read in front of the entire church with all your Christian brothers and sisters listening? How could you look those same people in the eye during fellowship afterward once everyone knew your problem? Euodia and Syntyche were probably especially embarrassed since they were leaders in the church. Obviously, Paul was saddened by their relationship and wanted them to change. We do not know what the problem was, except that they did not agree with each other. Isn't that how most of our problems begin?

In some relationships, one person may be the "obviously" guilty instigator. Other times, both are equally at fault but neither can see the other person's point of view. In Hannah's case, Peninnah clearly provoked her year after year. Peninnah seemed like a mean and extremely difficult person. Poor Hannah could not get away from her unless she also left her husband. Yet despite experiencing years of distress with no relief from the problem, Hannah did not retaliate or scheme to get back at Peninnah. As the favored wife, she could have bad-mouthed Peninnah to Elkanah (1Samuel 1:5). Instead, she took the "high road" and relied on God.

Of course, relief from difficult relationships usually does not come right away. Sometimes, we must wait on the Lord for many years. This is an extremely hard path—the same path that Jesus walked.

"He committed no sin, and no deceit was found in his mouth." When they hurled their insults at him, he did not retaliate; when he suffered, he made no threats. Instead, he entrusted himself to him who judges justly

(1 Peter 2:22-23, NIV).

You might be a witness to troubled relationships among your friends and family. Or you yourself might be in a challenging relationship right now. Every time you think of that one person, you cringe and your heart sinks. You may feel trapped by that man or woman, not knowing what to do or how to resolve your problem. You have tried over and over to resolve the relationship, but all your efforts seem to go nowhere. Some of us might have even left our homes or churches because the relationships were so painful and seemingly impossible to reconcile.

As I write this chapter, I am in the midst of helping three women restore their relationship with one another in the church. Each woman feels that her viewpoint is correct and none of the people involved sees the situation in the same way. For this reason, they asked me to help out as an objective party. As I've looked into the circumstances, in certain areas it seems fairly clear who was at fault. I can see how actions and conversations were unfortunately misinterpreted. On top of all of this, all parties have become emotional and have blown up at one point or another causing more hurt feelings and deep wounds.

When you are in the middle of such disagreements, it can be extremely hard to be humble and apologize especially after someone has made accusatory and hurtful statements. Those words sting and leave scars. Sadly we can never take them back nor can the other person quite erase them from her memory. Even if we say, "I didn't mean it that way"—the fact is that those unkind and sometimes cruel words come out in the midst of an emotional moment and their effects are lasting.

Peninnah's continual taunting deeply pierced Hannah's spirit, affecting her emotionally and physically. With a broken heart, she would weep and would not be able to eat. That is what hurtful words can do to a person. The Bible even warns how the tongue is a fire, a world of evil among the parts of the body. It can corrupt the whole person and is set on fire by hell (James 3:6).

But from we read about Hannah, she did not complain about Peninnah, nor did she gossip about Peninnah to her husband. In fact, Elkanah seemed oblivious to what was happening between his wives, because he thought that Hannah was only sad because of her inability to conceive.

Her husband Elkanah would say to her, "Hannah, why are you crying and why won't you eat? Why are you sad? Don't I mean more to you than ten sons?"

(1 Samuel 1:8, NLT)

An important lesson I have learned through the years is that I cannot change anyone else. Each person must decide to change him or herself. If the person doesn't see his or her faults, God will often bring about change through some big event or chain of events. Whether it is in marriage, in sibling relationships, partners at work or friendships, we can *gently* and *lovingly* bring up how we were hurt, but it is 100% up to the other person to determine whether to change or to continue to behave badly. I emphasize "gently and lovingly" because in the emotion of the moment, we can end up saying something that worsens the problem rather than helping it. Though the person might not show it, even seemingly "tough" women can be crushed by "temperate" words. If we are gracious in our manner, we may be able to influence change that could help the other person.

Hannah had a gracious manner. She chose to go to God and allow him to completely deal with the matter. She prayed earnestly for God to give her a child, and he did. She was vindicated through the power of God instead of through revenge or retaliation. Her difficult relationship actually pulled her closer to God.

In her prayer, it is clear what she felt deep down inside about Peninnah.

Hannah prayed and said, "My heart exults and triumphs in the Lord; my horn (my strength) is lifted up in the Lord. My mouth is no longer silent, for it is opened wide over my enemies, because I rejoice in Your salvation. There is none holy like the Lord, there is none besides You; there is no Rock like our God. Talk no more so very proudly; let not arrogance go forth from your mouth, for the Lord is a God of knowledge, and by Him actions are weighed. The bows of the mighty are broken, and those who stumbled are girded with strength. Those who were full have hired themselves out for bread, but those who were hungry have ceased to hunger. The barren has borne seven, but she who has many children languishes and is forlorn."

(1 Samuel 2:1-5, AMP)

Hannah was confident that God saw Peninnah's arrogance and that her actions were weighed and judged by him. Though she had been barren for years, Hannah eventually bore seven children while Peninnah languished and was forlorn. In other translations it says that Peninnah "wastes away," "pines away," and "becomes feeble." Evidently, her negative words and cruel attitude came back on her own head. Hannah did not have to lift a hand or speak a word of slander against her adversary—God was the arbiter and the judge.

Many times we like to take matters into our own hands, for retribution or for revenge. Some of us don't feel secure if we cannot take control of our lives, of people and of situations. Not a few of us like to have influence over our circumstances and strive to manipulate events so that things work out according to our desires.

For those of us who are mothers, we feel responsible for our children, so we often try to direct and dictate what is best for their lives. This, of course, is necessary when our children are small, but unfortunately, a few of us can even impose our opinions on them later in their adult lives. Moreover, this tendency to be manipulative or controlling can spill over into other areas of our lives. We try to change our boyfriends, our husbands, our bosses and our friends rather than trusting in God. We can become moral policemen by dictating, controlling and correcting them constantly.

Instead of controlling others, however, we are commanded by God to be self-controlled. Self-control is a fruit of the Spirit. The only individual you can control is yourself. The only person you should try to change is yourself. We waste so much time and energy trying to manage, regulate and run the lives of others—their behavior and their thinking, when it is simply not possible.

If we don't get what we want, we resort to nagging, pouting or even fits of rage. One of my daughters had the habit of pouting when she did not get her way. She would stick out her lower lip. We would often tease her about her lower lip getting "fat."

When we read about Samson and Delilah, it describes Delilah using pouting as a form of control.

> *Then Delilah pouted, "How can you tell me, 'I love you,' when you don't share your secrets with me? You've made fun of me three times now, and you still haven't told me what makes you so strong!" She tormented him with her nagging day after day until he was sick to death of it.*
>
> (Judges 16:15-16, NLT)

Unfortunately we can fall into unhealthy dynamics with our husbands, our friends and other significant relationships through such manipulation. I remember a time when I was "reminding" my husband to do something. I probably asked him about five times, thinking that he had forgotten my request. He was extremely patient each time I mentioned my desire, but after the fifth time, he looked at me and said, "Honey, I heard you the first, second, third, fourth and fifth time. If I don't do it right away, it doesn't mean that I forgot. It would be helpful if you reminded me up to three times. After that, if I forget something important, I will take all the blame." His humble appeal resonated with me, and I have kept to the three times and he has kept to his side of the agreement. In this way, I have felt his graciousness.

Hannah could have chosen to nag her husband and say, "Sleep with me more, so I have a better chance of having a baby," or "Why do you keep sleeping with Peninnah when she already has children? You should sleep with me instead!" By refusing to resort to manipulation, Hannah preserved a strong bond with her husband.

We can choose to allow our circumstances or people like Peninnah to affect our lives and our hearts, or we can live in the grace of God, forgiving them and letting God deal with them. In many cases, the more we insist on proving our point of view or justifying our way, the more we end up being upset and damaged in our faith. The point is not to always be right, but to always strive to be "righteous." Hannah remained righteous, and God blessed her humility and her grace.

In this modern world, our temptation can be to fight back, to make sure we get what we want or think we deserve. We want to drive our point home to ensure that the other person "*gets it.*" Ultimately, as we have established earlier, we have no control over others. It is God who raises up the humble and crushes the arrogant. It is God who brings justice upon the wicked. And God guards the lives of his saints so that he can be glorified in all our relationships, whether difficult or wonderful. Allowing God's grace to reign in our souls will guide us through our difficult relationships and will prevent Satan from using us to hurt the people that we love deeply.

The Incomparable Riches of His Grace

According to Forbes magazine there are over 1,500 billionaires in the world, and among them 172 are women.[1] Out of these 172 women, only 14 are self-made billionaires while the others inherited their wealth through widowhood or family inheritances. Perhaps two of the most well-known self-made billionaire women are Oprah Winfrey, the television celebrity, and Doris Fisher, the entrepreneur who started Gap.

You and I may not be billionaires in the world's eyes, but the Bible tells us that we have been blessed with incomparable riches through God's grace.

> *And God raised us up with Christ and seated us with him in the heavenly realms in Christ Jesus, in order that in the coming ages he might show the **incomparable riches of his grace**, expressed in his kindness to us in Christ Jesus. For it is by grace you have been saved, through faith—and this not from yourselves, it is the gift of God...*
>
> (Ephesians 2:6-8, NIV)

In other translations, it says: "incredible wealth," "exceeding riches," and "immeasurable riches." When we look at these billionaire men and women, their wealth and riches can be measured. Yet, the abundance that each of us has received in Christ far exceeds what these wealthy people possess in quantifiable assets. That is why his grace is so incredible.

Unfortunately, many of us look at billionaires like Oprah Winfrey and wish that life would somehow treat us in the same way—start out as a single mom with no money and make it big, so big that we do not even have to think about money any more. Though a few of us may experience this fairy tale-like life that we see on the news, alas it will not be a reality for most of us.

Despite the fact that we may not have millions of dollars, we can all rejoice, because each of us who has made Jesus Lord of our lives has experienced a "billionaire life" through his grace. God's grace has been lavished on us (Eph. 1:7-8). We have been blessed with eternal life and forgiveness for all of time. This wealth or riches far exceeds any material blessings in this life, because it lasts eternally. The possessions of this world only last in this lifetime and cannot go with us into the next world. Besides, who needs to bring gold and pearls to a place where those same materials are used to line its streets and build its gates?

Part of Hannah's problem was Peninnah, but the other part of her problem came from within Hannah herself—she desperately wanted children. It obsessed her thinking and affected her emotionally until she thought she would burst.

> When the sacrifice had been offered, and they had eaten the meal, Hannah got up and went to pray. Eli was sitting in his chair near the door to the place of worship. Hannah was brokenhearted and was crying as she prayed, "LORD All-Powerful, I am your servant, but I am so miserable! Please let me have a son. I will give him to you for as long as he lives, and his hair will never be cut."
>
> (1 Samuel 1:9-11, CEV)

Ladies, we have all had times when we wanted something really badly—so badly that we thought we were going to explode. We might have cried out to God and prayed about it over months or years. In our yearning, we might have even lost sleep over that one desire. Our desire may not have necessarily been selfish, but rather a deep need in our soul—whether for a child, for a college degree or for healing from cancer. Every woman has yearnings at one point or another. Since it is a part of our nature to *feel* deeply, we also *need* deeply.

Hannah wanted a child so badly that she was willing to give the child to the Lord for all the days of his life. She wanted the emptiness and the shame of being barren to be taken away from her. As a result, she was willing to do anything—even give up raising her child so that her disgrace would be taken away.

For many of us, this vow does not make sense. If she wanted a child, why would she give him up to the Lord afterward? Yes, it seems irrational as we read from our modern point of view. However, when we look at our own situations, things do not look as black and white. Haven't we all made foolish promises so that we could get something else in exchange? In the pages of the Bible, there are many examples of men and women who have desired to attain something and were led to make foolish promises out of their burning desires. The Bible warns us to think before we vow.

> *Don't fall into the trap of making promises to God before you think!*
> (Proverbs 20:25, CEV)

God wants to satisfy our longings and even promises to do so (Psalm 37:4). But this promise comes as a result of us trusting in him. An important part of trusting God is to see how he has already been faithful to us. When we truly comprehend all the blessings that God has already given us, we will be able see how very blessed we are, even apart from other deep yearnings being fulfilled. We do not have to burn with desire or be emotionally distraught over situations that we cannot control. Instead, we can live with gratitude in our hearts.

One of my dear friends, Lin, had the unthinkable happen in 2001. Her dearest and most precious love, her husband Barry, died as a result of a brain tumor. This tragedy began with a seizure in 1986, while they were living in Baton Rouge, Louisiana and serving in the full-time ministry. Through special treatments, God gave Barry the gift of life for fifteen more years. Unfortunately, the cancer returned with a vengeance in 2000, with little hope of recovery.

After mourning the death of her husband for several years, Lin began to pray for a husband again. She was ready to move forward. For what seemed like a long time, however, she did not see any answer to that desire on the horizon. During those years, Lin worked as a nurse and poured herself into raising not only her own children, but also into serving as a wonderfully caring mentor to many other women in her church. Her joyful reliance on God made her an example to others facing tough challenges, and she was invited to gatherings around the country as an inspirational speaker. As Lin's children all graduated from high school, and she became an "empty-nester", the desire to re-marry became a deep yearning in her heart.

In October of 2007, Lin's best friends, Mark and Diane, had just walked home after a nice dinner out with friends. Suddenly, Diane fell to the floor and passed away that same night from an aneurysm. For Mark, it seemed that the meaning of life had ended with the death of his beloved. He was wrought with sorrow and at times even lost the will to live. In his grief, the first person he called was Lin. Mark and Diane were lifetime best friends with Barry and Lin. The children in their two families were also knit together over the years. Lin became a crucial part of comforting Mark and Diane's children and helping Mark himself to heal his broken and grieving heart. Amazingly, they fell in love and were engaged.

On September 22, 2012, my husband and I had the honor of attending Mark and Lin's wedding. This wedding renewed, refreshed and strengthened my faith in ways that no other wedding had done up to that point. I witnessed a modern-day "Divine Romance." I watched my friend Lin walk down the aisle escorted by Brandon and Morgan, her two sons, to her waiting groom, Mark. Mark was like Isaac:

> *"Isaac brought Rebekah into the tent of his mother Sarah, and he married Rebekah. So she became his wife, and he loved her; and Isaac was comforted after his mother's death."*
>
> Genesis 24:66-67 (NIV)

During the wedding vows, Mark read a poem that he had written for his bride. It touched my heart deeply. It explained so much of what they had gone through apart and together. There wasn't a dry eye in the assembly. Even their children and their spouses shed tears while they watched their parents share their love for one another. All of their children were in the wedding party. Mark's son Matt was his best man. Lin's daughter Jordyn was her maid of honor.

After the wedding, we released helium balloons, each with a note of prayer for the newly married couple tied to the string. I believe that all those prayers are known and heard by God who was truly given the glory that day. Though their greatest desire during their darkest times was to go to be with their spouses, God granted them the yearnings of their hearts in his timing and in his wisdom, all to bring glory to him.

Dear sisters, as we look at our desires, longings and needs, God is also cognizant of them all, even if the answers to our prayers may not be exactly what we wished for. Nothing got past him unnoticed. He understood how badly Hannah wanted a child. He also saw the ways in which Peninnah treated her harshly, and how Hannah never made her situation an excuse to become bitter, envious or jealous. He knew how Hannah had turned to him in desperation. After her heartfelt prayer, I have a feeling that Hannah had entrusted her future to God and would have lived content with the other blessings that God had given her, even if she never had a child.

In the same way, God sees everything in each of our lives, including the unfulfilled longings of our souls. We, as women, need to see how rich we already are in God's sight and never lose sight of the immeasurable blessings we have in him. We are already much wealthier than any billionaire on this earth. Our inheritance is kept in a special vault where it will never spoil or fade or go away. When the right time comes, each of us will receive that amazing inheritance.

> *Praise be to the God and Father of our Lord Jesus Christ! In his great mercy he has given us new birth into a living hope through the resurrection of Jesus Christ from the dead, and into an inheritance that can never perish, spoil or fade—kept in heaven for you...*
>
> (1 Peter 1:3-4, NIV)

We are immeasurably blessed on earth, and a rich inheritance is waiting for each of us in heaven. Let us learn from Hannah to trust in God to give us the yearnings of our hearts as we learn to be content with the riches of his grace and love.

 QUESTIONS FOR THE HEART

1. Read 1 Peter 2:21-25. Have you ever been treated harshly by someone or teased because of a weakness in you? Pray to God that you will not

allow those words to replay in your mind any longer and adopt Christ's attitude despite the unfair treatment you are receiving or have received.

2. Relationships can cause so much heartache. Do you have a relationship that causes pain whenever you think of that person? Have you taken the "high" road and tried to reconnect with that person?

3. Pray daily for that person this week, just as Christ prayed for his enemies so that a lack of forgiveness does not rule over your heart.

Chapter 8

ESTHER: CHOSEN BY GRACE

Opportunities Through God's Grace

(Suggested Reading: Esther 1 & 2)

I have a beautiful and special friend named Mealea. She grew up amidst troubled times in Cambodia during the Pol Pot regime. "Pol Pot's army killed every member of my family. I have no one left," says Mealea, with tears streaming down her face while recounting this tragic episode in her life. Sadly, Mealea is just one of many Cambodians who have lost their entire families during the genocide that ravaged their country from 1975-1979. It is estimated that over 2,000,000 Cambodians were killed during this time, which was about 20% of the total population.

Much like the Nazi concentration camps, families were separated by sexes and age, then forced to do hard labor in the fields with little food under extremely unsanitary conditions. The children were forced to sleep in small areas where they were lined up similarly to the 19th century slave ships— alternating head to toe on the floor. They were given small pots to relieve themselves in but were not allowed to leave the room. The lack of consistent showers caused their hair to be matted and filled with lice.

Mealea recounts her experience during this time and says:

"I was a very young girl, eight years old, during the Pol Pot regime. My parents had been in another province called Siem Reap having been drafted for military duty while my brother and I were sent to a work camp. I lived with a group of children who were the same age. They gave us limited food, 3-4 spoons of rice per meal, only two meals a day. They made us work very, very hard every day with no weekend or rest for almost four years. We slept in camps that were wet with urine and stool. We had lice on all over our head and skin. The hardest part was that my whole family—my parents, one sister and two brothers—were all killed by the Pol Pot regime." As she says these words, she is choked up and almost unable to speak.

"I'm sorry. I'm sorry," she apologizes as she speaks. "It's just so hard for me to remember and talk about the most painful part of my life. I want to forget it all."

Esther's story began in 483 BC; 103 years after Nebuchadnezzar had taken the Jews into captivity. During that time, Xerxes had become the king. He was the fifth ruler of Persia from 486-465 BC. So imagine being a descendant of the captives in Persia—a slave, because that is who Esther was. She had no father or mother and was raised by her cousin, Mordecai. They could not have been very wealthy or have had high status in society. Basically, Esther was a "nobody" in Persia. But God had a better plan for her life.

Because Esther's parents both died when she was still young, Mordecai did his best to raise Esther during a very turbulent time in Israel's history. Her people had been taken as captives by the Persians. And she was a Jew; she was someone looked down upon by the Persians. The prospect for their lives was not promising, but opportunity came for Esther when she was chosen to go to the king's palace.

Sometimes, when we least expect it, God presents us with an opportunity. But our attitudes toward those opportunities can influence how we respond. Because Esther had experienced difficulties in life, it could have been easy for her to be bitter and angry towards her circumstances. Instead of being open to change in her life, she could have gone to the king with a pessimistic and negative attitude, believing she would never be selected no matter how hard she tried.

Negative experiences in our lives can cause us to become cynical regardless of the fantastic opportunities we receive. Instead of becoming excited, we start looking for the flaws, believing that our luck will run out sometime in the near future. Rather than embracing and enjoying the opportunity, we brace ourselves for the storm or catastrophe, which is waiting just around the corner. In this way, we often allow our pasts to dictate our futures, instead of the other way around. Open doors are what they are. They are not God's way of taunting us.

Even understanding this, some of us can still look at opportunities with suspicion, because we desire security. We cling onto "false" securities of money, status and relationships in order to guard ourselves from disappointments. Sometimes we sabotage our opportunities with our skepticism and mistrust. Whether we are aware of it or not, we search for ways to feel secure but do not find the security that we desire, because we refuse to see the possibilities.

Esther had a slim chance for stability in her life. She was at the mercy of the Persian government and its society. Though she was chosen as a prospective wife for King Xerxes, she had no assurance or promise that it would all work out for her. If she was not picked to be queen, she would have become a part of the king's harem, and that would have been the end of the story. Her life as an odalisque or concubine would have guaranteed her a life without a "real" husband and, quite possibly no children or a family of her own. After being taken into the king's palace, no other man would dare touch her without risking his life.

Based on Esther's background, she probably wanted a family and desired to be loved and cared for. But death had been a very familiar visitor in her life; taking away those she loved the most. However, by entering the palace, she was given the prospect of marrying the king—a possibility for a better life. Who would have imagined that she could be queen? Her sights were probably not as high as Mordecai's vision for her life. At that time, the king met with many maidens. Esther probably began to dream about becoming queen and leaving her sad life behind. It was the greatest opportunity of her life—a miracle even to be in the palace.

Esther was taken into the palace and chosen as a worthy suitor for the king. After months and months of preparation through beauty treatments and training, she was finally able to meet him. Imagine getting ready for a date over a span of twelve months knowing that in one single night your whole future would be determined. And like a miracle, the king chose Esther.

> *And the king loved Esther more than any of the other young women. He was so delighted with her that he set the royal crown on her head and declared her queen instead of Vashti. To celebrate the occasion, he gave a great banquet in Esther's honor for all his nobles and officials, declaring a public holiday for the provinces and giving generous gifts to everyone.*
>
> (Esther 2:17-18, NLT)

My friend Mealea had a grandfather who was just like Mordecai. He and her grandmother took Mealea into their home after her little brother and the rest of her family were murdered. They raised her until she was ready to go into the city of Phnom Penh for university. Though her grandmother passed away early, her grandfather continued to take care of Mealea through the years. Because of her grandfather's belief in her, she was able to get into a prestigious university in Phnom Penh. The opportunity came, and she decided to take it. After graduating, she acquired a job with the Ministry of Commerce as a unit officer, which is one of the highest ranks in the government.

Not only did Mealea secure a high paying job after having nothing for many years, but she also met one of the few doctors left in Cambodia. There were only a handful remaining after Pol Pot had slaughtered all the high officials, teachers, doctors and lawyers. Dr. Kim Meng Tan graduated from medical school in 1992, which was just thirteen years after Pol Pot was pushed out of power. When Dr. Kim Meng met Mealea, they fell in love. After many years of sadness and pain, she had met the love of her life, and they were married. That next year, there was a Christian mission team that landed in Phnom Penh to spread the gospel. During that time, both Kim Meng and Mealea made Jesus the Lord of their lives.

The result of all of Pol Pot's bloodshed has left Cambodia with a population of people in dire need of mental and physical support. Mealea and her husband have not forgotten the atrocities they saw in their childhood. As Christians, they made it their mission to help their people in every way they can, so that all their people can rebuild their lives.

His Grace Works Behind the Scene

(Suggested Reading: Esther 3 & 4)

A dream came true. Life was finally going to be different for Esther. There was even a public holiday declared in celebration of her marriage. The wife of a king. Residence in the grandest home in the kingdom. Servants to wait on her hand and foot. Horses and chariots to carry her throughout the countryside. The finest of all of Persia available at her fingertips. Freedom from the chains of society. A crown on her head. What more could anyone ask for? And she lived happily ever after right? Not quite. As soon as she was situated in her "cush" life—enter the villain, Haman. He was determined to bring down Esther's cousin Mordecai by destroying all of his people, namely the Jews. Once again, more death, more tragedy, more loss knocked on Esther's door.

But what would a story be like without a villain? In real life, Satan is always there to make God's people fall. Satan often uses arrogant and powerful people to help him accomplish his schemes. And what better person than Haman? A man blinded by hatred and self-importance who was bent on destroying God's people. More than that, he had influence over Xerxes as well. Yet, all this was not enough for Haman. There was someone in his life that vexed him, annoyed him and didn't respect him enough. And who was the source of his irritation? Mordecai.

> *When Haman saw that Mordecai would not bow down or show him respect, he was filled with rage. He had learned of Mordecai's nationality, so he decided it was not enough to lay hands on Mordecai alone. Instead, he looked for a way to destroy all the Jews throughout the entire empire of Xerxes.*
>
> (Esther 3:5-6, NLT)

It wasn't enough that Haman was placed in a seat of honor higher than that of all the other nobles (Esther 3:1). In fact, all the king's officials would kneel down and pay honor to Haman—all except Mordecai. This infuriated Haman. Mordecai, however, would not compromise his faith to make a man happy. For him to kneel before any man would have been a sin against his God.

Haman's fury led to an evil scheme. He plotted and planned. He decided to speak to the king and began the process of eliminating Mordecai and his people. He was not afraid to approach the king with the problem of the Jews and present the issue as if it affected the king and his throne. His vitriolic criticisms about the Jews convinced King Xerxes to sign the edict that would kill all the Jews (Esther 3:8-10).

Enter God's incredible grace. You see Haman didn't know that God was already working behind the scenes to put Queen Esther on the throne—long before his devious schemes would come to fruition. Haman was about to be surprised by the hand of the Lord. He did not understand that Mordecai worshiped a powerful and amazing Being—and that he would never be second to any man.

Mordecai was willing to give his life for God. He was a man of integrity, living to please and to honor God. If it meant to defame his Lord in any way, his title meant nothing to him. Compromise was not an option for Mordecai. He was not going to satisfy his egotistical superior. He was faithful to his Lord and would not budge or concede to please a man, especially not a man like Haman who was bent on self-glorification.

Haman could never understand having such devotion to a god, because he was focused solely on himself. He was his own god. He was consumed by jealousy. He did not want to share his glory with anyone. He desired to be respected, honored and worshiped by all people. He was addicted to his status and position. He was obsessed by his lust to have all the glory and admiration in the kingdom.

With Esther already on the throne, God's people had a chance to be saved. Esther had hidden the fact that she was a Jew from the king and his attendants. The past she was ashamed of would become the key to saving her people.

Dr. Kim Meng and his wife, Mealea, faced the same kind of corruption in the Cambodian government though more than a decade had passed since the Pol Pot Regime was defeated. Moreover, there was no hospital for him to work in, because they had all been destroyed during the Pol Pot regime. Dr. Kim Meng described the situation, "Upon graduation in 1992 from medical school, I became a doctor. I, however, had no hope at all to be able to practice as a true medical doctor, because there were two huge problems. One issue was that the government could not pay me enough salary to live on. They could only pay me about US$10-$15 per month. The second problem was that the hospital had nothing: no equipment, no medicine and no human resources. For this reason, I decided to stop working for the government and went to a private company working as a cement salesman. Later, I became a trade manager for Toyota. With this job, I could earn US $150 and later $450 a month."

During that time, my husband Frank, met a man in Tokyo named Bernie Krisher who knew of a building that a friend wanted to donate to establish a hospital in Phnom Penh. Since Frank was on the mission team to Cambodia, he was able to connect Bernie to a non-profit organization, HOPE Worldwide, to initiate this project. Frank and Bernie forged a friendship and worked with Dr. Kim Meng and Mealea to establish a hospital to help the people of Cambodia. There was much opposition from government officials who desired bribes and special favors, but Frank and Bernie were able to have an audience with the king of Cambodia, King Sihanouk, who helped them get the project off the ground!

When the doors of the hospital opened in December of 1996, Dr. Kim Meng and Mealea felt that their long-time dream had at last come to fruition. Through word of mouth, people flooded the doors of the hospital with crowds consisting of over 300 people every day. Many traveled from the provinces, which were located on the outskirts of Phnom Penh, pulling their sick family member in wagons and primitive carts. They would sleep outside the hospital for days waiting and hoping to get free care for their loved ones.

At just the right time, God placed Esther in a high position in the land to help his people. The Jews could have been destroyed at this time in history had it not been for Esther being queen. The Jews had been taken as captives by the Babylonians, and then placed under the rule of the Persians as the outcasts of society. It would have meant nothing to the king to destroy a people who were insignificant in his kingdom. But as a "reject" of society, Esther was placed in a position of honor—someone who sat next to the throne over all the land.

Over and over again, this is how God's grace works. His grace is revealed from behind a veil concealing and often obscuring a greater plan. What we may see before us may not be how God sees it. In his great wisdom and love for his people, he works behind the scene with his master plan accomplishing his will. Even the decisions that each of us make are a part of God's plan, *for it is God who works in you to will and to act according to his good purpose* (Philippians 2:13,

NIV). I love the literal translation: *for God it is who is working in you both to will and to work for His good pleasure* (Young's Literal Translation).

The Grace of His Marvelous Timing
(Suggested Reading: Esther 5-6)

It is interesting how Mordecai was very careful about protecting Esther throughout the whole process while the king was choosing his new wife. He advised Esther not to say anything about her nationality. In obedience to her cousin, Esther hid her past and her family background.

> *Esther had not told anyone of her nationality and family background, because Mordecai had directed her not to do so. Every day Mordecai would take a walk near the courtyard of the harem to find out about Esther and what was happening to her.*
>
> (Esther 2:10-1, NLT)

At God's timing, Esther was forced to reveal her background. What she thought would be the greatest obstacle to attain the throne had now become an asset for rescuing her people!

Imagine being Esther. She was faced with a choice. If she revealed her background, the king could have become angry and rejected her. After all that she had done to get to where she was, she might have lost it all—and at the risk of being accused of lying to the king. Everyone in the kingdom knew the story of Queen Vashti. She did not make the king happy, so she was dethroned and who knows what happened to her after that? It certainly was not an era of happy endings but a time of insecurity and fear, because at the whim of the king, he could take even a queen's life.

Today, if you met Mealea, you would meet a grateful woman of God, who serves and loves her people. Christ shines in her heart and in her family. She has three beautiful children who love the Lord. She is living the life of a queen now, never having to worry about food on her table or about the clothes she would wear. In fact, she has been blessed so much that she and her husband live in a grand home and donate a lot of money to the needs of Cambodia. More than that, she helps many women with their grief as they deal with their pasts. Though there is still pain in her heart when she remembers the past, she clearly sees God's grace having saved her life.

Similarly, Esther learned to embrace her past through a time when God called her. She fought through the challenges and relied on the Lord. She used her background, which she could have been ashamed of, to work for the good of others. Esther's heart was not focused on self-preservation but on the people she loved most.

Likewise, let each of us, through the grace of God learn to embrace who we are. At his timing, he will use the aspects of our lives we might have been ashamed of to be displayed for his glory. God has given us precious tools for our lives—even the negative elements of our lives are for his glory and not to our shame. Allow each one of these factors in our lives to become pearls of grace, which decorate our seemingly insignificant lives, with precious worth.

By the Grace of God We Are Who We Are

Whether we are in a position of influence and power or not, God has placed each of us exactly where he wanted us to be. This is the same in the church, as God has arranged the parts of the body, He has set them exactly where he needed them to be (1 Corinthians 12:18). It is by the grace of God that we are who we are. God does this according to his vast wisdom and his wonderful purposes. It has nothing to do with merit and whether we deserve it or not. We don't earn God's favor and salvation—nor do we ever deserve it.

In the same way, Esther did not earn her crown by her own accomplishment nor did she deserve it. Even though she went through twelve months of beauty treatments and worked hard to win the favor of Hegai, the harem manager—so did the other women who desired the same position. She gave her best to the king and, by the grace of God, pleased him immensely. She even won the favor of everyone who saw her—which was no small feat (Esther 2:15). But who gave Esther her beauty? Who made Esther's personality so attractive? And who influenced the minds of everyone in the palace? Who helped to sway the king's inclinations so that he would favor Esther out of all the women brought to the palace? Who else but God?

Many of us believe that we earn the right to be rewarded in one way or another, if we have worked hard to accomplish a task or some difficult undertaking. If this is the perspective we have on life, we can become angry or even resentful at God when we don't receive our "just reward" after all the effort. But this is not how God works. The world and its ways compensate for results after much toil. It lifts up individuals for their successes. It applauds those who by sacrifice and struggle earned their way to the top. Although we as Christians need to fight to be our best and to labor hard for his righteousness, we cannot live to "earn" our rewards.

Sadly, when we get caught up on the treadmill of needing recognition or desiring appreciation for our efforts, our hearts can fill up with all sorts of evil and negative thoughts. Those seeds of bitterness spread their roots and infect us without us realizing it, and we eventually become controlled by those emotions and thoughts. This affects our view of God and our opinions of others, building distrust and doubt in our minds. While doing this, we attempt to protect ourselves and our reputation, but our relationships become damaged as we build barriers toward others because, in our perception, we are not receiving the proper respect and honor we feel we "deserve".

God understands our needs. Through his grace, he has given us our abilities and our gifts—not to be wasted just on ourselves but to be used for the benefit of others as well. He has great plans for our lives—not to harm us but to give us a hope and future (Jeremiah 29:11). He is omniscient and omnipotent, and knows where to put his people so that they will be in the right places at just the right time (Acts 17:26). Nothing is done without the Lord's foreknowledge. Nothing is hidden from his sight.

After World War II, my paternal grandfather decided to start a business with his best friend. My grandfather was the president of the company, and they ended up making quite a lot of money. His partner and best friend wanted more, and that longing transformed into bitterness in his heart. He built up so much resentment toward my grandfather that he decided that he should have a bigger share of the company. One thing led to another and his greed for money and power turned into a decision to steal all the money from the company. One night, he went into the office and took all the company's money and ran off. They could never find him again. In the end, my grandfather almost ended up going bankrupt as a result of this event.

What was most painful about this incident was not the theft, but the friendship that they had supposedly forged over the years. My grandmother told me how they cried themselves to sleep many nights having seven children to feed and all their money gone in one night. She told me how bitterness and resentments were dangerous. They lead to all kinds of lies, greed and evil. I remember her telling me never to allow my heart to stray to that ugly place. She said that God sees all. My grandmother felt that through her oldest son, who is my father, she was vindicated, because he became a famous doctor and an extremely rich man. Until my grandparent's death, my father lavished them with the best he could give them, and my grandmother felt healed from the devastation of her past.

By the time Mordecai approached Queen Esther about the edict commanding the Jews to be destroyed, Esther had been queen for a few months or possibly a few years. It is not specifically mentioned, so we can only speculate. But life was good for her—a new home, a new husband and a position of influence. As she got situated into her new and luxurious life, it would have been easy for Esther to get the "queen" syndrome like Queen Vashti did, when she refused to come out and display her beauty before the king's court (Esther 1:12). But Esther was different, possessing a unique spirit of humility. She valued her relationship with Mordecai and never stopped listening to her precious cousin—even as queen of the land. The power and high status never went to her head. In fact, through Mordecai's guidance, she understood God had put her in the position she was in.

Haman, on the other hand, let his extraordinary status go to his head. He was promoted and raised to be the king's right hand. He felt that he deserved his high rank. So instead of remaining humble and remembering where he had come from, he reveled in his seat of honor. He wanted everyone around him to kneel down and pay him honor. His pride and arrogance took control of his choices. He got the "honor me" syndrome. For this reason, when Mordecai would not bow down and pay him honor like the other officials, he became incensed and bent on destroying, not only Mordecai, but all his people (Esther 3:5-6).

Haman's desire for self-glory grew and grew until he was blinded by it. He was obsessed by his desire to be recognized. At every turn, he was consumed by his title and his need to feel important.

When Haman entered, the king asked him, "What should be done for
the man the king delights to honor?" Now Haman thought to himself,
"Who is there that the king would rather honor than me?"

(Esther 6:6, NIV)

It is during this time that God began to set the scene to bring Haman down and to lift Mordecai up. God, in his infinite mercy, did not destroy Haman right away and gave him a chance to change and to have a different perspective of Mordecai. The king asked Haman to go around the town and to honor Mordecai the Jew throughout the city (Esther 6:10-11).

At this point, Haman could have changed his mind and decided to respect Mordecai more, but instead, he grew more resentful of Mordecai and was filled with grief over the situation.

Sin whispers to the wicked, deep within their hearts. They have no fear
of God at all. In their blind conceit, they cannot see how wicked they
really are. Everything they say is crooked and deceitful. They refuse to act
wisely or do good. They lie awake at night, hatching sinful plots. Their
actions are never good. They make no attempt to turn from evil.

(Psalm 36:1-4, NLT)

The road of the wicked is very tempting, especially when we feel unappreciated and under-valued. Even though some of us may be in a "higher" position in our companies or in the churches where we worship, we may not be satisfied by the measure of control we have or the amount of accolades we receive. This desire for self-glory, when unfettered, can blow up into an evil obsession that destroys not just the person herself, but all the people around her.

Instead of obsessing about how *we* are treated, we may need to think about how we treat others. I had a special friend named Etsuko, who is now in heaven with the Lord. She taught me a special lesson about this. She was the CEO of her company and a very devoted Christian. She told me that I should always watch how the people I respect treat the waitresses, the bellboys and the cashier—namely people that are not usually treated with honor. She said that the people, who treat those people respectfully and kindly are truly worthy of respect, because their true hearts are revealed by how they treat people of "lower" status, though they are not less because of their jobs. She told me she never did business with a person who treated the waiter or waitress badly or disrespectfully. In the end, Etsuko's comment made me examine my heart, as I had not deeply considered how I behaved toward those who served me. It does not matter how high our positions at work are or how much honor we receive in the end. What matters is what is in our hearts, and who we truly are inside.

When Mordecai and Esther were elevated into their positions of influence, they never allowed their characters to grow proud. Why? They were focused on honoring God. They understood that they had gained their position, not from within themselves, but through the grace of God. Because of this, they remained faithful and humble. When Esther heard about Haman's evil scheme, she did not hesitate to act, even if it jeopardized her life.

> *Then Esther sent this reply to Mordecai: "Go and gather together all the Jews of Susa and fast for me. Do not eat or drink for three days, night or day. My maids and I will do the same. And then, though it is against the law, I will go in to see the king. If I must die, I must die."*
>
> (Esther 4:15-16 NLT)

God gives us his grace through the power of the Holy Spirit, so that we can overcome the tendency to grow prideful in our inner beings. He sets himself against those who are arrogant and full of themselves. God gives grace to those who have a modest and respectful attitude, and he continues to bless them with his grace as long as they are humble enough to receive it.

> *But He gives us more and more grace (power of the Holy Spirit, to meet this evil tendency and all others fully). That is why He says, God sets Himself against the proud and haughty, but gives grace [continually] to the lowly (those who are humble enough to receive it).*
>
> (James 4:6, AMP)

When Haman was given power and influence, he misused his title to fulfill his personal agenda. With such strength, he could have done great things for his kingdom. Instead, he abused his status to write up an edict to destroy all the Jews in the land. His ambition drove him to convince the king to consent to a heinous act. God set himself against Haman, because his life was all about self-glorification. His conceit blinded him to the point of wanting to destroy thousands of people so that he could gain all the power in the kingdom for himself. Jesus says:

"What good is it for a man to gain the whole world, yet forfeit his soul?"
(Mark 8:36)

His grace helps us to overcome these tendencies in us. And everyone can fall into this temptation. Satan is proud and arrogant. The Evil One wants us to be haughty and take honor away from God. As long as man is credited for the wonders that God performs, then Satan wins the battle in this world. "Let us then approach God's throne of **grace** with confidence, so that we may receive mercy and find **grace** to help us in our time of need." (Hebrews 4:16, NIV) In the times we need a hand, God is able to work in powerful ways—not just in our lives—but also through us to impact others.

Never Giving Up
(Suggested Reading: Esther 7-8)

What makes you give up? Have you ever given up on something big? If so, why did you decide to completely give up? Were there times that you have persevered against all hope through a challenge? What kept you from giving up at those times? Are you overall a fighter or someone who easily throws in the towel? What helps you to push yourself to the very end?

Thomas Edison lived from the late 1800's to 1931. He was the youngest of seven children. As a child, he went partially deaf because of an accident. Despite this handicap, he became a prolific inventor and businessman who did not want to ever give up. He was awarded 1,093 patents for his life's work of inventions. There are many famous quotes made by Edison about not giving up.

"Many of life's failures are people who did not realize how close they were to success when they gave up."[5]

"I have not failed. I've just found 10,000 ways that won't work."[6]

"Our greatest weakness lies in giving up. The most certain way to succeed is always to try just one more time."[7]

Jesus showed us the way when he died on the cross. He was an example of perseverance through intense trials. He suffered through unfair treatment, through betrayal, through flogging and through the cross. No matter how difficult his situation became, Jesus never gave up. Jesus could have decided to give up and live for himself instead of dying for us all. But he instead chose to die for *our* sins.

> *Therefore, since Christ suffered in his body, arm yourselves also with the same attitude, because he who has suffered in his body is done with sin. As a result, he does not live the rest of his earthly life for evil human desires, but rather for the will of God.*
>
> (1 Peter 4:1-2, NIV)

Esther had a Christ-like attitude as she persevered through the trials in her life. Though Haman tried to destroy her people, she had the courage to bring Haman's evil plot out into the open. The king became angry with Haman and had him hanged on the gallows in front of Haman's own house. King Xerxes gave Haman's whole estate to Esther, which in turn, she gave to Mordecai (Esther 8:2). This could have been the end of the story. A happily ever-after life this time around, right? But it was not—not at this point for Esther and Mordecai.

The Jews were still slated to be killed according to the king's original edict. Though Esther's personal life was going better, the problem of the edict had not been resolved. Esther was not going to stop here. Instead, she remained unwavering in her resolve to free the Jews from the predicament that Haman had put them in during his life. This was no small task but one that would take all of Esther's energy and wisdom to accomplish.

Once again Esther went to speak to the king. This time she fell down at his feet, crying and begging, "Please stop Haman's evil plan to have the

Jews killed!" King Xerxes held out the golden scepter to Esther, and she got up and said, "Your Majesty, I know that you will do the right thing and that you really love me. Please stop what Haman has planned. He has already sent letters demanding that the Jews in all your provinces be killed, and I can't bear to see my people and my own relatives destroyed."

(Esther 8:3-6, CEV)

I love Esther's heart to save her people. Unlike Haman, she used her position to help others when she could have just focused on saving herself. Her heart went out to her people. She knew their suffering after having been ripped away from their homes and becoming captives. She saw pain and death as a child. She had heard stories about her family and others who were taken captive as well. She would not let go of her desire to help and did not give up until she could change the situation, not just for herself but also for all the Israelites.

Letting God's Grace Rule Rather Than Our Personal "Laws"
(Suggested Reading Esther 9 & 10)

One of my greatest temptations is to give up when it gets too hard. Several times in my life, I have wanted to give up on my faith, on God and on the church. During those times, I have doubted God's Word, lost trust in the brothers and sisters in my church, and wondered where I could hide to escape the pain. I would want to crawl into a shell and hide. In short, I don't like to suffer, and I search for a "happy ending" in every dark time. When I don't find the possibility of a good outcome, I can tend to give up. But God has given me strength over the years, through his Spirit, to believe and not to live by my ways but his ways.

The old way, with laws etched in stone, led to death, though it began with such glory that the people of Israel could not bear to look at Moses' face. For his face shone with the glory of God, even though the brightness was already fading away. Shouldn't we expect far greater glory under the new way, now that the Holy Spirit is giving life? Therefore, since God in his mercy has given us this new way, we never give up.

(2 Corinthians 3:7-8, 4:1 NLT)

What I have seen in my life is that I have a "law" of how my life is supposed to turn out. When my "law" is broken in a big way, I decide that I can't believe anymore in God's love and his goodness. Logically, I know that this thinking is ridiculous, but when situations do not work out as I expected, I become discouraged and doubt God's graciousness in my life.

For instance, I had a law about prayer: if I prayed enough about something, then things should turn out the way I prayed about it. This did not happen with my having children. After my fourth miscarriage, I was devastated that God was not answering my prayers the way *I* wanted. I realize now that life doesn't turn out exactly the way I pray, because it is not about my plans but God's plans. God is not a waiter waiting for my requests and then fulfilling my order when I want it.

Without us realizing it, we live under invisible laws that we have established for our lives. If we are good, then God will bless us. If we make the right decisions, we should not have to go through excessively difficult times. If we live to please God, then our lives should turn out better than for someone who is not a Christian. If we work hard and give our best, then we will succeed in most of our endeavors. Isn't this the way so many of us think? We do not realize that so much of the good is a result of God's grace and not from the "laws" that we have created in our minds.

When such laws do not work out for us, we can often become disillusioned and doubt God's love and faithfulness in our lives. Such a mind does not have room for God's grace. *So don't be misled, my dear brothers and sisters. Whatever is good and perfect is a gift coming down to us from God our Father, who created all the lights in the heavens. He never changes or casts a shifting shadow.* (James 1:16-17, NLT) We cannot allow Satan to deceive us into thinking that the "good" in our lives comes from *our* efforts and *our* faithfulness.

My best friend and mentor, Gloria Baird has taught me many important lessons through the difficulties she has had to endure. In May of 1963, Gloria gave birth to a baby boy named Gary Todd. Both Al and Gloria were thrilled with their first child. He was a "honeymoon baby" with Gloria getting pregnant during their honeymoon! After his birth, Baby Gary was having trouble breathing, because he was born a month early. He was diagnosed with

Hyaline Membrane Disease. Just days after Gary's birth, the unthinkable happened. He stopped breathing and died on the third day.

At the time, Al and Gloria wondered whether God was punishing them or whether they had some sin in their lives that God was unhappy with. They went through all kinds of emotions as they desperately tried to come to grips with what had happened. Just a few months later, the doctor told them they could start trying for another baby. In August of 1964, their daughter Staci was born. She was healthy and strong. They rejoiced with her birth.

God seemed to smile down on them with the birth of Staci. Later, however, on March 17 1966, Gloria gave birth to twin girls, Laura and Alicia. While Gloria was at the hospital, just twenty-four hours later, both babies passed away. They were premature births and also suffered from the same disease as their first son. In three short years, they had lost three babies.

Esther understood God's grace amidst adversity. She made a decision to make a difference and not give up under trial and opposition. Although life's troubles tried to knock her down over and over again, she remained tenacious in helping others rather than to fall into self-pity and becoming a victim of circumstances. After speaking to the king, Queen Esther had won the initial battle against Haman, but this was only the beginning for her. The Jews were still in danger of being destroyed by Haman's ten sons.

Esther learned not to be ruled by fear but rather to live by faith. This faith strengthened and inspired her to push forward. It gave her the motivation to never give in and fold under the evil influences of others. She wanted to make sure that Haman's control would no longer linger in the kingdom. For this reason, she had the ten sons of Haman condemned to death—a final and complete victory for the Jews.

> *The king said to Queen Esther, "The Jews have killed and destroyed five hundred men and the ten sons of Haman at the citadel in Susa. What then have they done in the rest of the king's provinces! Now what is your petition? It shall even be granted you. And what is your further request? It shall also be done." Then said Esther, "If it pleases the king, let tomorrow also be granted to the Jews who are in Susa to do according to the edict of today; and let Haman's ten sons be hanged on the gallows."*

So the king commanded that it should be done so; and an edict was issued in Susa, and Haman's ten sons were hanged.

(Esther 9:12-14, NASB)

My friend Gloria never gives up. With battle scars from losing her first child, then twin babies to the same disease. She fought through and ended up having three beautiful daughters who are all married to faithful Christian men, and they have children who love the Lord. But Satan was not done with her. Recently, Gloria was diagnosed with ovarian cancer. My mind went racing at the thought of losing my best friend, mother in the faith and partner in the gospel. For me to lose her would be worse than losing my right arm and leg!

I, however, watched Gloria have an attitude of strength and faith that made me feel ashamed of my lack of conviction in God's mercy. Moreover, Gloria maintained an unflinching sense of peace and trust in God that I felt was "unrealistic" at times. You see she was prepared and ready for whatever the outcome. She was surrendered to God.

I was not.

And there came the difference in our attitude toward God in same the situation. From the time of her surgery, which removed all her female organs, to the six chemotherapy treatments, which made her lose all her hair, Gloria drew me into a journey of learning to persevere with faithfulness alongside her. In my mind, this was one more "bad" thing that God put in my life. For Gloria, it was a way for God to glorify himself through her life.

With no hair on her head and her body aching from the damage of the chemotherapy treatments, Gloria kept smiling and encouraging others. She would attend church with an anti-bacterial mask on, so that she would not become ill with so many of her white blood cells destroyed, and she would hug everyone, reassuring them that God was faithful. She did not doubt for one moment that God was going to get her through this time in her life. Before and after every one of her chemo treatments, I would call her and her husband, Al. I would be nervous and anxious about the effects of the chemo on Gloria's body. She battled through month after month following each chemo treatment. She was going to do whatever it took to live and to serve God longer.

It has been over a year since her diagnosis with cancer, and she is now cancer free!

Esther and Mordecai worked together on behalf of their people. God gave them success, because none of it was for themselves. They went from a hopeless situation to one of triumph and safekeeping.

> *Mordecai the Jew became the prime minister, with authority next to that of King Xerxes himself. He was very great among the Jews, who held him in high esteem, because he continued to work for the good of his people and to speak up for the welfare of all their descendants.*
>
> (Esther 10:3, NLT)

This kind of victory only comes through complete reliance on God and believing in his grace. No matter how hopeless our situation may be, we should not despair. God is in complete control. He will give us the strength to overcome, if we put our trust in him. Neither Mordecai nor Esther was out for his or her own interests. They gave their best at every turn while trusting in God.

Al and Gloria have not wasted this past year as they traveled around the world doing marriage retreats and family conferences. They keep serving God even though they are past retirement age. They continue to give all that they can in order to help others. They have not wasted a minute of their suffering by giving up or giving in but have continued to trust in God. Through the grace of God, they are able to help many people. Their suffering was not without great effect on the lives of others. Their distress became a seed of strength to help others, just like Jesus' suffering for us.

Let us strive to be like Mordecai, Esther, Mealea and Dr. Kim Meng and Al and Gloria Baird by living in God's grace and surrendering to his plans and letting go of ours.

 ## QUESTIONS FOR THE HEART

1. Haman was blinded by his desire for recognition. This longing became an impetus for hurting many people. On the other hand, Mordecai and Esther never got a big head from their elevated position. Write out three

destructive characteristics of Haman and the three qualities in Mordecai or Esther that might have kept their hearts pure. When you look at the list you made, what similarities do you see in yourself?

2. Humility is a source of God's grace in our lives. His grace should help us to overcome our sinful tendencies. Write out a couple of your sinful tendencies that you would like to pray about this week. Take time out to pray about how they manifest in your actions and your attitudes.

3. Read these three Proverbs: Proverbs 11:2, 15:33, and 18:12. What are the patterns you see in humility and pride that you need to watch out for?

Chapter 9

MARY, THE MOTHER OF JESUS: SET APART BY GRACE

Highly Favored by God
(Suggested Reading Luke 1:26-56)

My paternal grandmother, who helped to raise me since I was eight years old, recently passed away. Oba-chan ("Grandma" in Japanese) used to sing me a song called "You Are My Sunshine." It was the only song she knew in English, and I used to love singing along with her. On her deathbed, she sang that melody to me in a frail whisper of a voice to let me know how much she loved me. Oba-chan also used to tell me that I was her favorite grandchild. She had twenty-three grandchildren, so whether it was true or not, I felt extremely special and favored.

When God sent an angel to Mary, he greeted her as one "highly favored"—not just once but twice! Upon hearing the salutation at first, Mary became anxious and unsettled. Of all the heroes in the Bible, Mary is the only one that God refers to as being highly favored. In effect, she was a favorite. We are not told why she was chosen over all the other women of her time, but God may have seen a remarkable integrity in her that set her apart.

In God's infinite wisdom, he had a plan to show his mercy to Mary. Does this mean she was perfect or even nearly perfect? Probably not. However, as we examine her life, we can certainly see an incredible attitude of humility and submissiveness toward God. She did not argue with the angel about what would happen to her reputation if she became pregnant. She may have worried about her future with her fiancé, but it is not mentioned in the scriptures. She may have fretted over how her parents might react, but she did not doubt God's plan. She had complete confidence in God's ability to work through her. The only reaction the Bible mentions is that Mary was at first disturbed by the angel's words, wondering what his amazing message could possibly mean.

Mary trusted the Lord though the consequences of being selected for God's plan could turn her life upside down. In fact, the world probably would not have considered her to be "highly favored" by God—especially with having to deal with a pregnancy out of wedlock during a time in society when unmarried women were expected to remain chaste. Sexual immorality was punishable by death for a guilty woman. An Old Testament scripture tells us the law of the time:

> *If, however, the charge is true and no proof of the girl's virginity can be found, she shall be brought to the door of her father's house and there the men of her town shall stone her to death. She has done a disgraceful thing in Israel by being promiscuous while still in her father's house. You must purge the evil from among you.*
>
> (Deuteronomy 22:20-21, NIV)

Even if Mary were to be saved from stoning, she might have borne a permanent mark of disgrace, particularly in the eyes of her own family and her fiancé's family. Imagine the response she must have received when she told her parents and Joseph about conceiving "God's child." After all, the angel had not revealed God's plan to them. They only saw that she was pregnant. Eyes must have been rolling in disbelief. Stomachs must have churned with outrage. Fear must have assaulted her parents who knew that their daughter could be stoned to death.

Moreover, how many women would want the responsibility of raising the Son of God? Mary was given a hard assignment that would require a lifetime of sacrifice, possible loss of friendships, moving far away from home and ultimately, heartbreak. From the world's point of view, she had been given a dishonorable task, not one that showed favor.

In all of this, however, Mary remained calm. Even days and weeks after the announcement of her pregnancy, Mary did not give in to panic or worry about what would happen to her. She did not suffer anxiety attacks as the "reality" of her pregnancy sunk in. Moreover, we see no evidence of her complaining to God or asking him, "*Why me?*" Rather, we only see her with complete peace and even excitement about the birth of her child, which are evident as she sings praises to God about haven been chosen to fulfill an honored task.

> *Mary responded,"Oh, how my soul praises the Lord. How my spirit rejoices in God my Savior! For he took notice of his lowly servant girl, and from now on all generations will call me blessed.*
>
> (Luke 1:46-48, NLT)

Despite the many challenging implications of her new role, Mary saw herself as being—not cursed or burdened with an unwanted and impossible task. She voluntarily submitted her entire life to God and his will. She considered her situation and said: "for the Mighty One has done great things for me; holy is his name." (Luke 1:49) Wow, how many of us would praise God given such a challenging task? Would we see ourselves as being blessed and given great things?

Mary was indeed favored by God. But for us, perhaps what's most impressive is that Mary actually saw herself as being favored. Despite her young age, she had an amazingly mature perspective on God's plan.

God's Favor Rests Not on Who We Are But What He Does

Mary described herself as a "lowly servant girl." She did not come from a prestigious family or a big city. Mary's hometown of Nazareth was a small town, not one of the major political or financial centers. It was, however, located along a trade route between cities. The population of Nazareth was probably somewhere from 100 to 500 villagers.[8] It was such an insignificant town that the Old Testament doesn't even mention it one time!

In God's infinite wisdom, family background, status, education or prestige were not crucial factors in how God picked the mother of his son. He obviously did not value what the world values. He did not choose Mary based on her credentials. He did not consider the amount of money that either Mary or Joseph possessed.

On top of this, God did not make life easy for Mary and Joseph. They had to travel a long distance while Mary was in the final trimester of her pregnancy. There was no place to stay in Bethlehem when they arrived. The young couple had to sleep in an animal shelter and their baby slept in a food trough belonging to those same animals—a less than ideal place for a newborn. I'm quite sure it was not hygienic by today's standards and not close to being comfortable for an exhausted, new mother.

Is this God's way of showing favor? The angel called Mary "highly favored," but is this how God shows his special grace to those whom he loves?

Our definition of being "highly favored" might be very different from what God had in mind. Delving deeper into the definition of this biblical phrase sheds some light on how God was operating through the various circumstances of Mary's life. A Bible scholar, David Grabbe, explains the spiritual definition of being "highly favored" in the following commentary:

> *The Greek word translated **highly favored** means "to grace," "to endow with special honor," or "to be accepted." The only other place it is used is, where Paul says to the church at Ephesus and to the body of Christ generally, "… to the praise of the glory of His grace, by which He made us accepted in the Beloved." From this example, we can see that being "highly favored" is not synonymous with being worthy of worship. Everyone in the body of Christ is highly favored because God has accepted us through the justification brought about by Christ's sacrifice.*
>
> *In verse 30, Gabriel tells Mary that she has **found favor with God**. "Favor" is the Greek word **charis**, which means "graciousness of manner or action." It indicates favor on the part of the giver and thankfulness on the part of the receiver. It is most often translated "grace" in the New*

*Testament. Gabriel tells Mary that she is the recipient of **charis**, of grace and favor by God—the emphasis is on what God is doing.*[9]

In effect, Mary being "highly favored" meant she was given God's grace and as the receiver, she was thankful. This didn't mean that God was going to provide Mary with a well-to-do or stress-free life. Rather, this blessing of grace was that God had chosen her and had accepted who she was even though she was an imperfect being. She was set apart to be the mother of his son through *charis*. This kind of grace was all about God, not about Mary and her qualifications.

Imagine a "perfect" child being raised by an imperfect mother. What pressure this would be. And what a daunting task! But at the same time, what an honor and privilege for Mary to be entrusted with his son. It would be harder on God's part, a perfect being, to give his perfect child to a sinner and a flawed human being. Only through God's grace was this young and inexperienced woman able to birth and to raise God's Son!

Herein lies the good news for all of us in Christ: each one of us has received *charis* (favor) from God. He has chosen us, as limited and faulty beings, to be children of a perfect God. We have been shown special favor, not because of who we are or what we have done or accomplished, but because of our faith in him. Therefore, grace should never become a millstone that we drag around in our lives as an obligation we now have to repay by filling our schedules with a myriad of "spiritual" activities. But rather, his *charis* should be a source of strength and confidence, knowing that we are loved and valued—favored in his sight.

As I mentioned briefly earlier in the book, I have a disease called Systemic Erythematosus Lupus, an autoimmune disorder where my antibodies attack its own body tissues. I have suffered hair loss, lesions all over my body, lung and liver damage, weight loss, fatigue and migraines for nearly twenty-five years. At times, I also experience debilitating pain and intense fatigue. When I was just twenty-seven years old, I could have lost my life to this disease as it had aggressively attacked my lungs and liver.

During that period, many people fasted and prayed for my life to be spared and for my health to be restored. I am forever grateful for every individual who did so. At the same time, since most of my friends were young and healthy, very few of them knew what to say or do to help me through those months and years that I fought for my life. My loving husband was also at a loss when it came to keeping me encouraged and hopeful. I constantly battled guilt within myself as I could not go to church or serve alongside my husband to minister to our young church planting in Japan. I felt angry with my body for not being able to "perform" as it should. There was so much to do, so many people to save and so many obligations to fulfill including taking care of my young daughters and husband. I was an "active" woman trapped in a sick and useless body.

To top it off, I had a personality that derived its self-worth from my ability to perform and produce results. Needless to say, since my body didn't work, I often found myself in the depths of depression. I felt that I had nothing to show for my faith or for my love for God. It was like a terrible nightmare from which I could not wake up. If you can visualize a tiger that has been able to roam free in the wild all its life and is suddenly put into a tiny cage, that is exactly how I felt. I could not understand why God would allow someone who wanted nothing more than to serve him in a foreign country to be completely paralyzed and incapacitated from carrying out his mission.

At that time, if someone had told me that I was loved and highly favored by God, I probably would not have believed that person. There was nothing in me that felt loved, favored or even liked by God during that time. I would have more readily believed God was punishing me and wanted to "teach me a lesson" through my misery. Day after day, I prayed for my body to heal, only to be met with "unanswered" prayers. This was not like the cold or flu—It was never going to go away. The doctors had told me: *I'm sorry, but hopefully with some medication, we can keep the symptoms under control, since there is no cure.* Day after day, those words echoed in my mind as I laid in bed.

However, looking back at those years when there appeared to be no hope, I see there was a transformation began in my heart to surrender to God's will for my life. I started to accept that perhaps the plans I had for my life were completely different from His plans for my life. What I had seen as a curse became a blessing.

How does a disease become a blessing? It brought me closer to my husband, my children and my friends. My condition created a bond of love and appreciation in all my relationships as each of us faced the possible culmination of my disease.

Family times were cherished. Meals together became special occasions, as I could not come downstairs to eat very often. Birthdays became treasured events, because we weren't sure how many we would have in the future. (To this day, we still strive to make birthdays extra special in our family.) No day, experience or time together was taken for granted. Without my sickness, I might have been running around in every direction and neglecting the people I loved the most and perhaps forgetting to make every day count.

My illness was, in fact, a gift from God. His *charis* allowed my husband and I to build a family that did not take each other for granted but appreciated every moment together. It became an impetus for me to start writing letters to each of my children every year on their birthdays, so that they could know how much I loved them at every stage of their lives, not knowing if I would be with them for their next birthdays. I gave that collection of letters to my oldest daughter on her wedding day. I made the letters into a memory album with photos and comments. We both cried together as we read through the letters remembering every year we were blessed to share together. I did the same for my second daughter on her wedding day as well.

Before my disease dominated my life, I thought that the harder I worked for God, the more "blessings" I would receive—meaning life would be easy, and I would rarely have to face serious difficulties or troubles. *Living God's way, life would be one blessing after another.* Or so I thought. Blessings did come my way, but in a very different form. His *charis* had a different shape in my life. No one looking from the outside would have ever thought that God was favoring me at all.

Not only did my family grow closer, but as I slowly began to recover through natural medicine, vitamins, herbs and organic foods, I learned to cook in a healthier way. Instead of instant macaroni and cheese, I made organic salads, fresh soups and whole grain breads and rice at a time when no one around me knew about health food.

By the time my children were in elementary school, they thought that rice, bread and sugar were all brown. One of my daughters even had an argument at school with a friend about the color of sugar and rice being white or brown! In the beginning, health food did not taste good to me or to my children, so I had to create and invent my own recipes to make the food more palatable. This experience prepared me to eventually teach a cooking class using all original Asian fusion recipes. I, currently, use my classes as a way to raise money for a school in Cambodia.

Being *highly favored* does not mean that we will have easy lives. Mary's life was not carefree. She had to travel away from her family while being pregnant for the first time, give birth in a stable and flee to another country then watch her son as he suffered disgrace. Her life was arduous—full of unexpected turns, taking her to places that her family never ventured to go. The quiet and simple life of Nazareth became a distant dream after God gave her the perfect child. There were costs and sacrifices that both Joseph and Mary had to make throughout their lifetime.

What does it mean for each of us to receive God's charis? Are we also truly "highly favored" by God?

> *For he chose us in him before the creation of the world to be holy and blameless in his sight. In love he predestined us to be adopted as his sons* **(and daughters)** *through Jesus Christ, in accordance with his pleasure and will—to the praise of his glorious grace* **(charis or highly favored)***, which he has freely given us in the One he loves.*
>
> (Ephesians 1:4-6, NIV, emphasis added)

In effect, this scripture tells us that we are God's favorites. How? We were chosen before the creation of the world and predestined '*in love*' to be God's daughters. This is quite an honor and privilege. Yet, this does not mean that our lives will be trouble free. Those tears you still shed for that lost child, that pain in your heart from that one horrible accident and that aching grief from the loss of so many loved ones might not completely disappear until we are called heavenward.

But we have an amazing hope before us, both in this life and the one to come. And did we do anything to deserve this? No, we didn't. God favors us for no apparent reason except that he cares for us. We were set apart by God's choice. He loves us as his daughters, because it was his will and his plan.

As we go about our lives today, let us try to imagine God singing to us: "You are my sunshine, my only sunshine, you make me happy when skies are gray. You'll never know dear, how much I love you. Oh, please don't take my sunshine away."

Take heart, dear sisters, for you are much loved and "highly favored." So be filled with thankfulness in your heart to God.

I Am Blessed; You Are Blessed; We Are Blessed!

I love gifts. When I was a young teenager, just thirteen years old, I remember my father inviting a designer jeweler to our home. The merchant brought what, at the time, amounted to about a million dollars worth of jewelry in five large briefcases. (Today, that same jewelry would be worth several millions.) He opened briefcase after briefcase of sparkling rings, bracelets and necklaces, all the best in their class. My father told my mother to choose whatever she wanted. Then to my surprise, he looked at me, smiled and told me to get whatever I wanted, if I saw something I liked. After looking through every display, I picked the smallest and most simple ruby ring.

My father looked at me with a look of disappointment and said, "Is that all you want?"

I nodded shyly not knowing why he was disappointed with me. But I was guessing that he wanted me to get something bigger and nicer.

In reality, I liked the smallest ring, because it fit nicely on my finger, but my father thought I was restraining myself, so that he would not have to spend much money on me. So he pulled open one of the other suitcases and proceeded to choose four more rings and asked me, "Do you like this one? How about this one? What about this one? And this?"

When I nodded 'yes' every time, he told the jeweler, "We'll take all five of these for my daughter."

I looked at him in shock and said, "Daddy, I don't need all those rings. I'm fine with just this one!"

He insisted, and he handed me the rings in their special red velvet boxes with the biggest smile on his face.

I will never forget that day.

Today, I am wearing the ring he bought my mother that night. She passed away just a few years later and on the day of her cremation, my father took the diamond ring off her finger and put it on my finger with tears in his eyes saying, "This is yours now. She won't need it anymore."

God is generous with his gifts and blessings. If my earthly father would want to lavish me with such beautiful jewelry, imagine what God is willing to do for us having the earth at his feet. And that is exactly what God has done for us. He has not only given us his grace at the cross, but he has also given each of us every spiritual blessing in Christ.

> *Praise be to the God and Father of our Lord Jesus Christ, who has blessed us in the heavenly realms with every spiritual blessing in Christ.*
>
> (Ephesians 1:3, NIV)

When Mary was told that she would give birth to the Lord's child, she did not worry and argue with God asking, "Why did you make me pregnant at this time? Don't you see what bad timing this is? Now Joseph won't marry me!" She did not panic and say, "Now the town will stone me to death. How will I prove that it was you, Lord, who made me pregnant? They will think that I am mad!" She did not reason with God about his timetable begging to change his plans, "Lord, could you wait a few more months until I get married? Then, it won't look so bad if I'm pregnant a little early."

Instead, when we look at Mary's prayer, we see complete and utter confidence in God. She called herself blessed. She recognized how through the grace of God, she was given a child and that all generations would call her blessed. The blessing motivated her, spurred her on and gave her the strength to be brave in the face of the challenges ahead. She submitted herself to God's will and called herself the servant of the Lord.

We, too, have been blessed. We have received so many blessings and gifts from God. Sadly, we are often unaware or forgetful of this fact. At times, we do not appreciate the blessings that we have in Christ, because we focus on the "what if's" of life:

> *"What if" I can't pay the mortgage this month because my car broke down and I need to fix it?*

"What if" I get fired because of that stupid mistake I made?

"What if" I don't get good enough grades, will I still get into my dream medical school?

"What if" I never get married?

"What if" my cancer treatments don't work this time around?

We worry about money, school, bills, jobs and family. Our eyes get focused on what we see: the "curses" of life rather than the blessings of God. We see problems, obstacles and all the negatives of our lives. But God has given us special favor and abundant blessings.

What are these blessings? They start with Christ's love and daily forgiveness. They extend to the gift of the Holy Spirit. They expand even further with the spiritual gifts. Furthermore, we have the gift of having a personal relationship with the King of kings and the Lord of lords. Through Jesus, we have the blessing of our spiritual family here on earth. And if that wasn't enough, God has given us the promise of heaven where we will live in eternity with our Father forever and ever.

If you asked me why my father suddenly lavished me with such wonderful gold rings, I could not tell you why. I had not been especially good that week. I do not remember doing extra chores so that he would reward me. I know that I had done absolutely nothing to deserve such expensive and wonderful gifts.

In the same way—but even better—God blesses us, not because we are perfect or because we have done something super-human and wonderful. In the New Testament, the word "blessed" possesses the sense that God is giving special favor with an emphasis on the spiritual blessings and gifts, which results in joy and prosperity. Its root is from the word *makarios* meaning fortunate, to receive benefits or receiving favor[10]. We are his children, so he wants to lavish us with gifts and blessings in our lives.

In the same way, blessings don't come because we did anything special or because we read our Bibles longer that week. Maybe you have recently experienced the blessing of a child, a promotion or an inheritance. We can give credit to ourselves, thinking that it's because we were "good" this past year. Or we can give the glory to God who blesses us, because he loves us, though we don't deserve it. And for those of us who have been blessed with the ability to play music, sing, dance or speak in front of large audiences, those gifts are also for God's glory and not just for ourselves.

More than talents, he also provides spiritual gifts. No one gift is better than the other. But the greatest spiritual blessing that we have received in Christ is, of course, the forgiveness of sins. What was the cost for that? It was the life of his Son. But God did not stop there. He continued to shower us with even more gifts.

> *Now there are varieties of gifts, but the same Spirit; and there are varieties of service, but the same Lord; and there are varieties of activities, but it is the same God who empowers them all in everyone. To each is given the manifestation of the Spirit for the common good.*
>
> (1 Corinthians 12:4-7, ESV)

> *We all have different gifts, each of which came because of the grace God gave us.*
>
> (Romans 12:6, NCV)

God in his infinite wisdom decided to give us different gifts according to his plans and his set foreknowledge.

> *The New Testament term "spiritual gifts" is literally "the spiritual supply of gifts." The word "gifts" is the English rendering of the Greek noun charismata. From this, some groups (that is, charismatic groups) get their name. It is formed from the Greek word charis, which means grace. So there is a very close association with grace here. The gifts are the physical manifestation of grace, visibly seen in a person's action and in their mind.*[11]

The Bible says that, "*In him we have redemption through his blood, the forgiveness of sins, in accordance with the riches of God's grace that he lavished on us.*

With all wisdom and understanding." (Ephesians 1:7-8) There is no such thing as a free gift, because ultimately *someone* has to pay the price. When we go to a store and receive a "free" gift, the merchant is giving it to you at a cost to him. When people give us presents, they had to spend money to buy them for us. In the same way, every spiritual blessing we have in Christ comes at a price to our God. And when God gives us gifts, he *lavishes* them on us. He is not cheap or sparing.

Dear sisters, let us rejoice just like Mary for the wonderful gifts that we have been given, starting with the forgiveness of our sins. I am blessed. You are blessed. We are all blessed in countless ways. I am so thankful that God is not stingy or miserly.

> *Praise be to the God and Father of our Lord Jesus Christ, who has blessed us in the heavenly realms with every **spiritual blessing** in Christ.*
> (Ephesians 1:3, NIV emphasis added)

Standing at the Foot of the Cross
(Suggested Reading: Matthew 27:11-61, 1 Corinthians 1:18-31)

Though my life with lupus has taught me numerous valuable lessons and has been a source of many blessings, it took me a very long time to see this. I went on an extensive and seemingly endless spiritual and physical journey. After living with the disease for several long years and with little hope of ever living a "normal" life, I stood at the foot of the cross and wondered why my life had turned out so differently from what I had expected.

In my mind, I could not erase the feeling that I was a burden to my husband, to my church and to my young children. Most of all, I believed that my life was a complete waste. I was of no help to anyone. Death became an almost attractive option for me. Jesus called me to carry my cross daily, but I had never imagined this kind of a cross.

My life was not supposed to be like this at all. I would have much preferred to bear the cross of culture shock, sleepless nights helping others, or crying tears for the lost souls around me as I labored in the mission field. I had given everything to Christ, but what did I get in return? An unproductive life that only caused worry and sadness for those who loved me the most. They watched me as my body and my spirit deteriorated month after month and year after year.

Most of all, I noticed that my children, when they were two and four-years-old, began to draw away from me and go to my husband for everything. I was not fun to be around nor was I able to provide for their needs. As a result, I had a weak relationship with my girls. Instead, I was a pitied object. "Don't bother Mama. She's feeling sick." "Be quiet and don't wake up Mama." "Don't jump on Mama, because it hurts her body."

More than simply my personal pain, Frank had to watch me day after day not knowing how long I would live. He would sit beside our bed and stare at me with sad eyes, which made the pain in my heart grow even worse. At times, the doctors would express doubt about my recovery, which was a distant dream for our family at the time.

Imagine Mary as she stood at the foot of the cross. Her son suffered and cried out to God, but there seemed to be no answer. What must have been going through Mary's mind? While her son hung in agony, did she watch with absolute trust in God? Or did she doubt God and become angry? Was she tempted to question the goodness of God? Or was she somehow able to hold onto an unwavering faith in God's power to work out this horrible situation? No matter what her thoughts were at the time, Mary probably could not see the over-arching grace that would come of Jesus' sacrifice. The astounding truth behind the cross would not be unveiled until days later. In any case, she was a witness to the greatest story ever told. And she was a key part of it.

Before we can truly understand what Mary's thoughts and feelings must have been like, we need to acknowledge that Mary was first and foremost a mother. Whatever might have been happening spiritually or emotionally to Jesus on the cross, Mary saw it from a mother's perspective. She saw and experienced the cross of Christ in a very different manner than all the other people onlookers or all those who would later become Christians. It was certainly one of the most difficult days of her life. There is no mother who can stand to watch her child suffer before her eyes. More than that, an angry crowd cursed her child as he died. Her personal reality and her pain were quite different from even the disciples or his siblings.

All of us will stand at the foot of the cross at one time or another. What Mary saw before her was death, suffering and a sad ending. Her eyes did not see that

God was granting all of mankind a new "beginning"—the start of his incredible grace. The greatest miracle was about to happen, but she did not recognize God working at that moment. Just like the cross, there may be a time in our lives that may appear to be a tragedy or a hopeless situation. What we don't realize at those times is that these moments can transform, and in fact, become the catalyst for God's greatest miracle.

As Mary stood at the foot of the cross, she might have wondered what she could have done better or how she could have helped her son. Her heart was pierced with indescribable sadness and agony.

And yet…

All the while, the cross was Jesus' ultimate victory and finest moment. Unknown to Mary, before her very eyes, the cross would be the event that would grant eternal life for all who would accept Jesus as their Lord and Savior. However, what she saw that day was not the true spiritual reality of the moment. God's grace was being fulfilled in all its glory, and Satan was defeated as Jesus breathed his last breath. There was no failure or defeat for her son. In the midst of her deepest sorrow, Jesus had won the victory on the cross, scorning its shame, and he sat at the right hand of God that very day.

When we look at the cross, there is no worldly logic or reason that can explain what happened. It cannot be defined by human wisdom, because it is all about faith. To all the bystanders and spectators, the spiritual truth was clouded by the fact that Jesus was condemned to die a criminal's death. He had *failed* his mission as the "King of the Jews." They saw the nails in his hands and feet. They heard the mockers as they taunted him and urged him to come down from the cross. The ones who were loyal to him mourned his death but probably believed he had not succeeded in bringing salvation to the Jews.

Yet all of them were wrong. They saw Jesus on the cross and registered failure when, in reality, they were watching the greatest victory possible for mankind. There was an invisible spiritual battle occurring as Jesus struggled against various temptations to sin all the way to the very last second—which is all it would have taken—and he would not have been worthy to die for our sins. Satan shouted loudly into Jesus' ears through the belligerent crowd. But Jesus overcame. Satan incited his disciples to desert him and one to betray him, but Jesus stood firm.

He defeated Satan and brought salvation to all humanity. And God raised him from the dead three days later.

> *The message of the cross is foolish to those who are headed for destruction! But we who are being saved know it is the very power of God. As the Scriptures say, "I will destroy the wisdom of the wise, and discard the intelligence of the intelligent."*
>
> (1 Corinthians 1:18-19, NLT)

God's grace cannot be seen through worldly wisdom. It cannot be understood through feelings or emotion. It is not something physical that we can see or touch. It cannot be studied through reason and logic. It can only be seen through the eyes of faith, which reveals its truth. No amount of education, study, knowledge or degrees can help us to understand the power and victory of the cross.

> *For since in the wisdom of God the world through its wisdom did not come to know God, God was well-pleased through the foolishness of the message preached to save those who believe.*
>
> (1Corinthians 1:21, NASB)

It is a blessing that we don't have to be geniuses to comprehend the cross. He chose the weak things of this world, the lowly things, the despised things, the things that are not. (1 Corinthians 1:27-29) *So where does this leave the philosophers, the scholars, and the world's brilliant debaters? God has made the wisdom of this world look foolish.* (1 Corinthians 1:20, NLT) Before God's eyes, we are wise, because we believe.

Many of us heard the message of the cross growing up, but it took time for us to see and to understand it. For some of us, we never heard the message of the cross until we were adults, and it still took time to really digest its meaning. For others, it may have taken just a short time to comprehend the sacrifice of Christ. Yet even after we grasped, at times, our spirits may drift and fall into unbelief.

Now that my illness is under control, I am able to travel and speak to different women. So many women who approach me have thanked me for remaining faithful despite my illness and for persevering through tragedy. They tell me how they were inspired to never give up. Very rarely has anyone told me that the sacrifice and hard work I did in the mission field was an inspiration. From my perspective, my illness and the tragedies in my life were not a topic of inspiration or of great faith, but a long chapter of excessive failure and wasted years. It is humbling for me to see how my hours of greatest weakness and despair are seen as a time of victory and heroic effort in the eyes of others.

But isn't that how we see the cross? At the most defenseless and vulnerable point in Christ's life, we see the most heroic and inspiring event before our eyes.

All of us will stand at the foot of the cross at one time or another. Just like Mary, there may be a time in our own lives the situation or series of events may appear to be a tragedy or a hopeless situation. What we don't realize in these moments is these experiences can actually become the catalyst for God's greatest miracles.

Is there something happening in your life right now that has blocked you or distracted you from grasping the whole picture of the reality of God's grace? Maybe you are experiencing difficulties beyond what you can bear. As a result you have grown stale in your appreciation of the cross. Take heart, dear sisters. Just like Mary at the cross, no matter how disheartened you feel now, the truth is that God's grace is at work within us.

After the resurrection, Mary no longer saw Jesus as simply the child whom she gave birth to but recognized him as her Lord. She saw him face to face and realized the truth. She stopped being just a mother, and as a servant to the most high, she bowed down to worship Jesus as the King of kings and the Lord of lords. She gathered with the apostles and prayed constantly with them.

"Death, where is your victory? Death, where is your pain?"—Hosea 13:14 Death's power to hurt is sin, and the power of sin is the law. But we thank God! He gives us the victory through our Lord Jesus Christ. So my dear brothers and sisters, stand strong. Do not let anything move you. Always give yourselves fully to the work of the Lord, because you know that your work in the Lord is never wasted.

(1 Corinthians 15:55-58, NCV)

Because of life's troubles, we can lose heart and begin to believe that there is no happy ending in Christ. In reality, Satan's world isn't supposed to have happy endings. I think about how the ending of my story could have been very different, if I had become bitter and turned away from God. There were many days when those temptations dominated my thinking. Satan wanted nothing more than for my story to end horribly.

In the same way, whatever you are facing right now, Satan wants you to believe there is no possible "happy" ending. And what we may perceive as an "ending" is not the end until we are gone from this world. Satan may be whispering in your ear. He may be, at times, shouting at you like he did to Jesus as he hung on the cross. But Jesus has already won the victory for you. You are not a failure. Your life is not a waste.

Sometimes, life does not make sense. Tragedy hits hard. Its pain can be unbearable. But just like Mary, let us hold onto the bigger reality of God's grace and not allow anything—even divorce, sickness or death—to sway us from the truth. Let us cling to God's reality and not be blinded by Satan's lies. We have received an amazing gift at which we need to continually marvel and share with others.

 QUESTIONS FOR THE HEART

1. Read Ephesians 1:4-6. Do you see yourself as chosen? Remember back to the moment that you became a Christian. How did God work in that situation to bring you to him?

2. Gifts are a way that God shows his grace to us. All of us in Christ have gifts that we can share with others. Write a list of the gifts you have in Christ. Which of these gifts are you presently using to build up the church?

3. At one time or another, we will stand at the foot of the cross and experience suffering both in those we love and in ourselves. What are incidents in your life that have helped to shape and mold you to see Christ better? Write a paragraph about that incident. If it has been recent, maybe you do not see how God has used it yet. Pray for God to reveal the spiritual reality to you.

Chapter 10

JESUS: HIS RADICAL LOVE CAN HEAL US

Jesus and His Grace

My Buddhist and Shinto background never taught me a proper view of God. He was omniscient…but so were all my ancestors. He was a mountain…and also a single boulder. He was the sun, the moon and the stars. He was every mammal and insect that roamed the earth. My image of God was a mixed up hodgepodge of animistic images and philosophical concepts—until I read the Bible and saw the real Jesus.

Even though I had grown up in America, no one had really explained to me all the incredible qualities of Jesus. So until I became a Christian in college, my impression of Jesus was entirely different from my friends who had grown up going to church. In fact, "my" Jesus resembled Buddha. When I was baptized into Christ, I knew and understood the important basics of Jesus, namely about the cross and salvation—but there was so much more that I still needed to learn about my Savior.

As a young Christian, I wanted to learn and to know every aspect of who Jesus was. I studied my Bible intensely and fervently. In many ways, I was playing catch up to my peers who knew the Bible better than I did. And as I absorbed the different scriptures on Jesus, I saw an overwhelming theme that did not exist in the religion I had grown up with....

That theme was grace. This grace was expressed through love that was overwhelming and, most of all, healing to me.

Jesus Loves Women and That Means You
(Suggested Reading: John 8:1-11)

Jesus loves you! Yes...you.

At a time when men and society showed little respect for women, Jesus loved and respected them deeply. He showed them their value by taking the time to converse with them. He chatted, ate and drank with them. When a sinful woman washed Jesus' feet with her tears and anointed them with oil, the Pharisees criticized her, but Jesus responded with appreciation and forgiveness. When he walked through crowds who eagerly pressed in to see him, he felt the touch of a single, desperate woman's faith and stopped to speak to her as a special individual.

When the crowd condemned a woman snatched from her illicit lover's arms just moments before, Jesus did not judge her (John 8:3). According to the law, she deserved to be stoned. Although he had the right to cast the first rock—being the only one present without sin—he did not. He would have been justified to sentence the woman, but he did not. He did not argue with the teachers of the Law or the crowd. He did not berate the woman. He did not excuse her sin, and in his grace, neither did he condemn her. He knew religious men were using her as a pawn to trap him (John 8:6). Jesus saw through their conniving spirit, acknowledged the woman's guilt, and granted her unmerited favor.

About a month after my mother's death, I traveled to Japan for her burial. During the Buddhist burial ceremony, my maternal grandmother pulled me aside and asked, "Your mother was with you the day before she died. What did you say that made her kill herself the next day?" My eyes widened in disbelief at the accusation, and I simply replied, "I tried to encourage her and begged her not to hurt herself. She has been suicidal for years."

My grandmother's eyes narrowed with suspicion as she made a final comment before the start of the funeral procession. She muttered, "You always brag about being a Christian. Why, then, couldn't you save her?" Those words stung so deeply that they were the only words I remember being said for the rest of the day. They echoed over and over in my mind as I watched my mother's ashes carried to her final resting place. I was already hurting and mourning from my loss, but my grandmother's words burned a hole through my already fragile heart. They emotionally maimed me for years.

Yes, what did I say to her to make her kill herself? Why do you keep denying the responsibility you have in your mother's death...and your miscarried baby's death? No one really knows how bad you truly are. Why are you even claiming to be a Christian? You are a hypocrite. You don't deserve to have his grace. Your grandmother was right. You are useless and worthless as a Christian. You couldn't even help save your mother. And you did absolutely nothing to save your baby.

Ugly words echoed in my mind as I read my Bible. They haunted me during my prayer times even as I knelt alone in the silence of my room. In addition to my grandmother's accusation, my own thoughts added many more criticisms that resounded in my brain like clanging cymbals, piercing my conscience with words like: *murderer, executioner, condemner.*

Many times, I would sit with my husband and with others to explain my feelings of guilt and regret, but those feelings never seemed to dissipate. I felt worse than the adulteress or the sinful woman. I was convinced that no one was worse than me. I could almost feel, at times, Jesus telling me, "Away from me you evildoer. I never knew you."

Certain events can sometimes cause us to believe we are beyond "fixing." We can often feel broken, damaged or disregarded. We try to hide our shame, and then we cross our fingers and hope Jesus will still love us, while deep down inside, we don't trust that he will. We can't imagine such immense compassion and mercy, because we hate ourselves or are disappointed in who we are.

The women who approached Jesus did not come to him in their perfection, but rather in their pain. They did not come in sufficiency, but in need. They did not stand before him as successful people, but as failures craving another chance. When we bring our wounded souls, our disappointments and our pain to Jesus, we can trust that:

His love is unconditional.

His grace is unending.

His forgiveness is without limit.

There is no human relationship that compares to this quality of love and the depth of grace that Jesus feels towards all women.

Recognizing Christ's Love and Grace
(Suggested Reading: Luke 7:36-50)

Jesus died for all of mankind—and as we've seen through the pages of this book, mankind doesn't just mean men. He died for us women who struggle with insecurity. He died for us women who have been adulterous. He died for those of us who have been abused, or raped, or victimized through injustice. He died for those of us with black, brown, yellow, red and white skin. He died for those of us who are rich, poor and middle class. He gave us his unconditional grace through faith in him, no matter what our background, race or talents.

Why, then, do we still struggle with "feeling" his grace and his love? Why is it so hard for us to truly recognize and experience his redemption and mercy?

When we became Christians, we stood before the cross and accepted his amazing grace to wash away our sins. Then after becoming a Christian, we may have gotten caught up with the "do's and don'ts" of our walks with Christ. We can end up focusing exclusively on the "cost of discipleship" and neglect to continually deepen our understanding of his grace. Though it is vitally important for us to obey his commands and to be committed to the lordship of Christ, we can never lose sight of the very core of our faith—his unconditional grace.

Grace does not stop at the point of becoming a Christian, but continues until we see our Lord's face in heaven. Think about the most unlovable women in the gospels. Who are they? *The sinful woman, the Samaritan woman and the adulterous woman.* These are women that Jesus could have easily judged and condemned. Instead, he forgave their sins and gave them salvation when they least deserved it.

I had to see that my relationship with God was not about my perfection, but in fact, my failures and sins had brought Jesus into my life. Jesus approaches the hurting, the sinful and the despised. Rather than shunning such people, he was a friend of tax collectors, drunkards and sinners (Matthew 11:19, NIV). Instead of scorning the rejected, he touched their lives and spent time with them. Instead of denouncing the disregarded or keeping a distance from them, he healed them. Instead of degrading the spurned, he lifted them up.

> "A bruised reed he will not break, and a smoldering wick he will not snuff out till he has brought justice through to victory. In his name the nations will put their hope."
>
> (Matthew 12:20-21, NIV)

Jesus never takes a damaged person and attempts to crush her. Nor does he take a weak person and seek to reject her. Instead, he tries to give her hope through his love.

After my mother's funeral and for many years afterward, I needed to erase my grandmother's words of reproach and replace them with Jesus' words of affirmation. Just like the sinful woman and adulterous woman, I had to choose to move on, at peace with God and with myself. This, however, was not an easy process. It did not happen overnight. In fact, it took years of fighting my invisible "demons", so I do not expect anyone reading this to easily experience healing if you've also been scarred by hurtful or abusive words.

Let us begin with an important fact that we, as women, need to accept regardless of our circumstances: Jesus loves us and *wants* to forgive us. There is nothing that can separate us from the love of Christ:

> Who then is the one who condemns? No one. Christ Jesus who died— more than that, who was raised to life—is at the right hand of God and is also interceding for us.
>
> (Romans 8:34, NIV)

If each of us would just accept Jesus' love, as well as the fact that he is interceding on our behalf, we can walk with confidence and joy in our lives. The scripture above tells us that Jesus is not condemning us. Moreover, Paul expands his thoughts with this list: neither *angels* nor *demons*, neither *death* nor *life*, neither the *present* nor the *future*, nor any *powers*, neither *height* nor *depth*, nor *anything else in all creation* can separate us from the love of Jesus. (Romans 8:39, NIV, emphasis added)

Take ahold of that thought and never let it go. Recognize and appreciate that his love and grace are real and are working in your life right now. Nothing can take his grace away.

Jesus Accepts All Who Come to Him
(Suggested Reading: Luke 8:40-48, John 4:4-26)

Who were they? The gospels refer to many women only by general description, such as the sinful woman, the Canaanite woman, the bleeding woman, the woman at the well, and the adulterous woman—their names are otherwise unknown. It is interesting to note that while many men with "less significant" roles in the gospels are specifically named, but these women remain nameless. We know them only by their gender and by their sins. But Jesus showed unbelievable patience and mercy to each of these special women. They are, in fact, a reflection of each of one of us.

Throughout the gospels, Jesus always responded with compassion and grace towards women. He ministers to them gently and never harshly. He responds to them kindly and with deep compassion, welcoming them when they approached him. Even as his mother stood at the foot of the cross next to the apostle John, Jesus' last request before his death was to ask John to take care of her. His first appearance after his resurrection was to the women who mourned for him as they came to his tomb.

To Jesus, women were never second-class or less important than men.

Jesus doesn't pick and choose whom to love and whom to forgive. He is willing to forgive anyone who will simply **come** to him. He told the sinful woman that her sins were forgiven and that her faith had saved her (Luke 7:50). Jesus gave her grace and salvation. To the adulterous woman, Jesus said, "Then neither do I condemn you…" (John 8:11).

Too often, we submit our minds to Satan's lies, which tell us we are not good enough or that we have failed to the point of no return. As a result, we distance ourselves from the Lord, believing that we are too far gone. Moreover, we do not even dare approach Jesus for fear of rejection. Instead of going to him, we grow farther and farther away from the one who can actually save us.

After being affected by my grandmother's accusation for many years, I remember reading these words from Jesus: "Then neither do I condemn you." Although I had read this verse before, I could not really *hear* what Jesus was saying, because I had been listening to the words of Satan instead. I had allowed Satan to use my grandmother's words to torment me when they really had no power at all. *I* was the one who had given them such destructive influence over my life.

I decided to believe that Jesus accepted me as I was, no matter how much I had fallen short. Only God knows whether or not I could have somehow prevented my mother's death or my baby's death. However, the fact is that Satan had planted lies in my mind. I had to choose to take back the confidence that Satan had stolen from me when he deceived me into believing his accusations. He had been whispering evil words to me for many years.

> *"He was a murderer from the beginning, not holding to the truth, for there is no truth in him. When he lies, he speaks his native language, for he is a liar and the father of lies."*
>
> (John 8:44b, NIV)

But now Jesus was saying to me loud and clear,

> *"The thief comes only to steal and kill and destroy. I came that they (you) may have life, and have it abundantly."*
>
> (John 10:10, NSRV)

Jesus acknowledges my weaknesses. He knows that I fall short. I can relate all too well to the Apostle Paul's fight against his sinful nature when he said,

> *I have discovered this principle of life—that when I want to do what is right, I inevitably do what is wrong. I love God's law with all my heart. But there is another power within me that is at war with my* **mind**. *This power makes me a slave to the sin that is still within me.*
>
> (Romans 7:21-23, NLT)

How did Paul overcome his struggles, imperfections and sin? His victory came through Jesus Christ.

> So letting your sinful nature control your **mind** leads to death. But letting the Spirit control your **mind** leads to life and peace.
>
> (Romans 8:6, NLT)

I had to *intentionally* fill my mind with the words of Christ and decide to let go of the destructive words that had caused me so much pain. Through much prayer, I received strength from Jesus. As a bruised reed and a smoldering wick, I went to him over and over again so that the Spirit could help me until I no longer heard those ugly accusations in my mind. I spoke out loud to Jesus in my prayers and decided to believe that he accepted me as I was. After doing this multiple times, my damaged soul was restored to peace and security in God's grace.

What words still haunt you? What events still replay in your mind over and over until they take control of your thoughts? How has Satan played with your memories and twisted them to work against you? Have you gone to Jesus to get help through prayer and through specifically and intentionally fighting those thoughts?

Today, those negative cycles have finally stopped. Now, I can remember my grandmother and reminisce about a kind, but imperfect woman, who helped to raise me during the years my mother suffered from her illness. I am so grateful for the ways she took care of my little brother and me into my teenage years. I miss her very much and wish she were still alive today, so that I could really thank her for all she did for me.

Ultimately, I realized that my grandmother was grieving over losing her daughter, and in her pain, she had lashed out at me, not meaning to hurt me. At the time, her personal sorrow was considerably more than she could bear. As a result of that experience, and because Jesus was able to heal the deep wound inside of me, I have learned to see hurting people beyond their destructive words and actions.

Jesus Wants a Special Relationship with You
(Suggested Reading: Ephesians 1:3-14)

It was Thanksgiving morning, and my husband and I went up to Daniel's Park, a spot near our home with a majestic view of Colorado's Rocky Mountains. We quietly offered a heartfelt prayer of thanksgiving to God, for he had brought us through a very challenging and stressful year. Nearby and unaware of our presence, our oldest daughter Miyoko, along with her two sisters, was perched on a huge rock outcropping. As they gazed upon the mountains under the pristine skies, they were enjoying their own thanksgiving devotional, offering prayers of gratitude to God.

We were not the only ones hidden from their view that morning. The location had been carefully pre-arranged, and Jason, Miyoko's boyfriend, was hiding a few feet away in the trees. In his hand, he held a beautiful diamond ring. As the girls finished their prayer, Jason left his spot and walked up to them, completely surprising Miyoko. While Frank and I watched from a distance, he got down on one knee and proposed to her, surrounded by the glory of God's creation.

Needless to say, Miyoko responded with a resounding, "Yes!" It was a moment of great joy for all of us (and perhaps a great relief for Jason). Just then, Frank and I received a text from our other daughters to come and join them. We had brought champagne, orange juice and croissants to celebrate the occasion.

Our daughter's eyes twinkled with absolute joy. She would not let go of her new fiancé's arm, holding onto him with a happiness that was contagious. At the age of twenty-six, she had, at last, found the man of her dreams. Jason glowed with pure exuberance as he smiled at his future wife. That look on his face melted my heart, because I knew there was now a man in my daughter's life that loved her as much as my husband and I did. Totally confident in Jason's love for her, Miyoko told me that it was the happiest day of her life.

When we are fully loved by someone who pledges his life to us, it is a joyous feeling. As Christians, we pledged our love to Jesus, and he promised to be in our lives, not only in this lifetime but also into the next. It is a promise that he does not make frivolously. He thought about it, planned for it and sacrificed his life for it.

Any relationship is a two-way street. However, our "two-way relationship" with Jesus originated from his direction. He reached out to us *first*. He called us to him *first*. He chose us *first* (Ephesians 1:4). He predestined us to be adopted as his children *first* (Ephesians 1:5). Through his blood, and not ours, we have received the riches of his grace on his initiative (Ephesians 1:6). We were at the time living in our sins and following the lies of this world. Our lives were dictated by the rules of Satan, separated from grace. Jesus proved his love for us by demonstrating that love when we were at our very worst.

When Jason went to pick out a ring for my daughter, he wanted to give Miyoko the finest ring he could afford. He wanted to demonstrate his love for her by giving her the most he could offer. Giving his very best represented his commitment to her.

Nothing on this earth can compare to Jesus' sacrifice. What he gave was beyond comparison. If we sat down and truly imagined Christ's love for us, we would be overwhelmed and filled with so much joy. It would be like heaven on earth.

I believe that heaven is going to be "heaven," because we will feel and experience the fullness and completeness of Christ's love in our souls. There will be no doubt, no skepticism, no fear or uncertainty. We will know without a shadow of a doubt that Jesus loves us beyond imagination. It will be the happiest day of our lives…and it will never end.

Jesus' Radical Love Heals
(Suggested Reading: 1 Peter 2:21-25)
Often, our pain and our hurts cloud and distort our understanding of love. Some of us have even been told it was out of love that something awful was done to us as children. For this reason, in our minds, we confuse Jesus' love with what we have seen and experienced in our lives. We compare, we doubt, and then we assume the worst.

But Jesus' love is different from the love of this world. He does not use, accuse or abuse women. He often rebuked his disciples, but he never spoke harshly to the women around him, no matter how sinful they may have been. Instead, he communicated with them tenderly, sensitively and lovingly.

How, then, do we erase our twisted image of love and replace it with the pure love of Christ after years of abuse? Can we accept his love when there is still a lot of pain and hurt inside? Is it truly possible to embrace the love of Christ and find healing in it?

"'If you can'?" said Jesus. "Everything is possible for one who believes."
(Mark 9:23, NIV)

We are called to believe—not the lies of this world, but *his* truth, which liberates us and obliterates the lies that cloud our thinking. He knows every hurting part of us, and he continues to envelope us with his unconditional love. In fact, he wanted to make sure that we would truly believe in his love by being willing to undergo a radical act of sacrifice in which he experienced unbearable pain himself.

*When they hurled their insults at him, he did not retaliate; when he suffered, he made no threats. Instead, he entrusted himself to him who judges justly. "He himself bore our sins" in his body on the cross, so that we might die to sins and live for righteousness; "**by his wounds you have been healed.**"*
(1 Peter 2:23-24, NIV)

According to this scripture, his wounds can and will heal us.

On January 17, 1995, an earthquake with a magnitude of 7.2 hit the city of Kobe, Japan. There were more than 6,000 deaths and over 30,000 injured. It destroyed more than 150,000 buildings and left about 300,000 people homeless.[12] Amidst the rubble, a woman and her two-year-old daughter were trapped under a building for nearly three days. In darkness, they waited and waited for help to come their way. During that time, the little girl became extremely thirsty. Almost completely immobilized by the debris, the only thing the woman could do was to take a piece of broken glass and slice her arm so that she could allow her daughter to drink her blood. This went on hour after hour, in the dark at various times of the day when her daughter would cry out with thirst. The woman was desperate to keep her daughter alive. By the time the rescuers finally found them, the mother had cuts all over her arms from desperately keeping her daughter alive without food or water within reach.

Imagine if the two-year-old had refused to drink her mother's blood. The little girl would have probably died of dehydration. But the daughter trusted her mother and believed whatever her mother said, and so she was able to survive.

You see, Jesus did the same for us. His blood is what keeps us spiritually alive. It never ceases to forgive us of our sins. It continues to cleanse us of all impurity. It helps us to survive this world and its temptations. But the condition is that we need to be like that two-year-old daughter, accepting and believing in that love. It may not be exactly how we would envision it. In fact, the little girl probably wanted apple juice or water, not her mother's blood to drink. Yet, for the little girl, it was essential for her survival—literally the gift of life.

Many years later, I do not know how the story has turned out for this little girl's life. As I write these words, she is most likely a young college student. I wonder if she remembers her mother's love for her during that horrific event. Does she believe that her mother loved her more than her own life? I wonder if she is grateful whenever she sees the scars all over her mother's arms—especially the ones that will never disappear because they were so deep—deep enough to pour out blood to quench the thirst of a two-year-old.

Wouldn't it be tragic if the daughter did not remember the event at all, or doubted her mother's story about what had happened during that earthquake? Imagine if the little girl grew up into a rebellious teenager who did not believe her mother loved her, and she ran away from home and rejected her mother. How would her mother feel after all she had done for her daughter?

Love can drive us to extreme measures. And just like that mother who was desperate to save the life of her child, Jesus was compelled to give a sacrifice that was so radical and extreme no one could ever doubt his love for us. There is no greater act of love than laying down your life for another. Grace is not cheap at all, but rather priceless and immeasurable.

Therefore, let us cut away the chains of the world's deceit and the doubts that entangle us, and let us embrace forgiveness through Jesus' sacrifice as the ultimate proof of his love. He is there with us, in us and beside us. He forgives us each and every day of our lives. Allow his love to mend those parts of your heart that no one else can heal.

I pray that from his glorious, unlimited resources he will empower you with inner strength through his Spirit. Then Christ will make his home in your hearts as you trust in him. Your roots will grow down into God's love and keep you strong. And may you have the power to understand, as all God's people should, how wide, how long, how high, and how deep his love is. May you experience the love of Christ, though it is too great to understand fully. Then you will be made complete with all the fullness of life and power that comes from God.

(Ephesians 3:16-19, NLT)

You Are the Bride of Christ

On May 5, 2013, our daughter, Miyoko, stood at the altar dressed in pure white with a veil over her beautiful face. She was elated to face Jason and profess her marriage vows to him. It was the moment she had been waiting for since the day that Jason had asked her to marry him.

Minutes later, after she and Jason had said their "I do's", Miyoko received her *very first kiss on the lips*! Before her relationship with Jason, Miyoko had dated steady with a few other Christian boyfriends. During that time, as a committed Christian, she had a deep conviction to keep herself completely pure until marriage—and had even decided not to kiss a man until her wedding day.

Personally, that first kiss was the most magical moment of her wedding, because it symbolized God's special grace to me. Even though I had lived a sinful life before becoming a Christian, God had given me a do-over through breaking a cycle of immorality that had existed in my family for several generations. That day, I saw a beautiful twenty-six-year-old woman give an absolutely pure life to the man of her dreams—something that I would have wanted to do with all my heart, but because of my own sin, was not able to do.

Thankfully, my friend Pat Gempel told me those many years ago that through grace I was a virgin in the eyes of God. And now, the pattern of sin had at last been finally broken through the power of Jesus. I was seeing the blessings of his grace being lavished on me at that very moment. It was the most beautiful kiss I had ever witnessed in my entire life!

You are the bride of Christ. He has taken you as his betrothed and lavished you with his grace. Paul refers to how the Corinthians were betrothed to Jesus:

For I am jealous for you with the jealousy of God himself. I promised you as a pure bride to one husband—Christ.

(2 Corinthians 11:2, NLT)

In Ephesians 5, the marriage relationship is compared to our relationship with Jesus. Even in the Old Testament, God refers to his people as his bride:

As a young man marries a young woman, so will your Builder marry you; as a bridegroom rejoices over his bride, so will your God rejoice over you.

(Isaiah 62:5, NIV)

Jesus is at your side as your bridegroom, and he will watch over you. He will protect you. He will rejoice over you. He will labor to keep you pure. He will toil to guide you safely through this journey in life.

*"…if we walk in the light, as he is in the light, we have fellowship with one another, and the **blood** of Jesus, his Son, **purifies** us from all sin."*

(1 John 1:7, NIV)

As Jesus' bride, we have been given the precious gift of the Holy Spirit. With his Spirit in you, you are provided the power to break the wicked cycles that have existed in your family, even for generations. You don't have to be the third generation of yet another divorce. You're not condemned to be the next generation of bitterness, unforgiveness, or adultery in your marriage. You're not destined to become yet another generation in bondage to addictions. Instead, through the grace of Jesus, you have been given the amazing gift to change and break the sinful patterns that have existed in your past.

"…for everyone born of God overcomes the world. This is the victory that has overcome the world, even our faith. Who is it that overcomes the world? Only the one who believes that Jesus is the Son of God."

(1 John 5:4-5, NIV)

This doesn't mean that if you have experienced divorce, Jesus is not working in your life. It doesn't mean that Jesus is not guiding your life if your son or daughter did not decide to walk in the path of the Lord. Likewise, if you battle with addiction, this doesn't mean that Jesus is not protecting you.

Following Jesus and his Word does not guarantee a perfect life, but Jesus does shield us from the overwhelming attacks of the evil one. *"We know that God's children do not make a practice of sinning, for God's Son holds them securely, and the evil one cannot touch them."* (1John 5:18, NLT) As we walk in the path of the Lord and do our best to present ourselves as a pure bride, Jesus holds us tightly in his arms so that Satan cannot hurt us beyond repair.

Jesus' Grace Gives Us a "Do Over"

As I mentioned previously, I have experienced four miscarriages. I would pray over and over for a healthy child, but the prayers were not always answered as I had hoped. Because of these events, I have had to fight to not be controlled by fear and dread. I eventually found out after my third miscarriage that the issue was my lupus. Apparently, my disease kept the fetus from developing properly. According to my doctor, the fact that I ended up with three healthy children is somewhat of a miracle.

When I consider all my tears and prayers during that time, I can also see how Jesus reached out to me, bearing in himself the sufferings that I experienced, and showing me the hope to overcome. When my anger overwhelmed me so much that I even cursed my life, I saw my Lord allowing himself to be cursed on the cross and yet, overcoming through his love and the power of his resurrection. When I felt in bondage to a sickly body, I remembered how Jesus submitted himself to be bound and even tortured in order to give me mercy, a gift I didn't deserve. Nothing I had experienced was beyond his empathy and power.

What I saw most was that Jesus transformed my mess and my anguish into a message of hope when I continued to be faithful and refused to bow down to Satan. Instead of letting go of my relationship with my Lord, I decided to cling on tighter. He told me in tender whispers:

"Come to me, all of you who are weary and carry heavy burdens, and I will give you rest.

(Matthew 11:28, NLT)

Often as women, we ask *why?* We want to know why something happens the way it does, but frequently, there is simply no clear answer. When we get up to heaven, maybe we can ask the Lord, and he will make it clear to us. Conversely, through my grief and affliction as well as those of others, I have seen how God works in difficult times to help others. In other words, I have seen how the Lord has used those tough times in my life to bring glory to himself and to encourage others who suffer in the same way. I have also comprehended how his grace is all surpassing and merciful, especially during the hardest times. I have appreciated the ways that Jesus has shown me mercy in my blackest moments.

We live in a world of broken relationships, divorce, adultery, addictions and abuse. In fact, I have many friends who are afraid to marry because of what they have seen and experienced. For those friends, being a bride did not have the same dreamy, fairytale-like feelings as it did for my daughter who grew up witnessing a fulfilling marriage so she expected the same for herself. Yet, I have also seen women who are incredible Christians believe against all odds in their Lord through challenging marriage relationships. Their mess has become a message of hope for me, because they remained faithful to Jesus and decided to push past their terrible experiences while holding on to the promises of Christ.

I have a dear friend named Vanessa who met a fun-loving and talented man at church. This man was devoted to God, and he had an ambition to serve in the ministry. The senior minister, an experienced former missionary, trained this young man to preach and to lead in the church. From every angle, this man seemed perfect for Vanessa. They had known each other for six years, and then she dated him for almost a year before deciding that he was "the one." They kept their relationship pure and received extensive pre-marital counseling. They had a beautiful wedding—her dream wedding. Nothing seemed to be amiss in their blissful beginnings. However, six months after they were married, her husband would disappear late at night to supposedly get together with people who needed his help. His wife never questioned his whereabouts since he was training to be a minister for his church. Over time, however, his stories began to unravel and not make sense—but even then she didn't doubt the discrepancies and continued to trust him.

Later, as these unexplained absences persisted, Vanessa felt hints of suspicion in her heart as pieces of their furniture disappeared and large sums of money were removed from their bank account. When she probed her husband about these things, his explanations were seemingly altruistic: *Someone was in trouble and needed the money. A family was in need of a television so I gave it to them, and we can buy another one sometime later.* No one would have suspected or guessed there was a web of deceit and lies that he had woven over the past weeks to justify all of his actions.

Several concerned friends finally intervened and inquired about his strange behavior. He finally admitted to the senior pastor that he had been selling personal items and using up their money to support his drug addiction. As a result, he entered a drug rehab center to get help, but gave up after only ten days in the program. When Vanessa found out that he had given up and that he had also been unfaithful to her, she decided to divorce him.

Vanessa was devastated. She felt betrayed, helpless and torn apart. In her mind, she could not grasp the reality of the situation and thought there must have been some misunderstanding. She lived in shock and disbelief for several weeks, often staring at the empty spot beside her in bed. Many mornings she would wake up and believe that her life was just a bad dream, only to realize the nightmare was a reality. She could not imagine how her beloved could do such horrible things. In a matter of months, those vows of love at the altar had become meaningless.

Vanessa wrestled many times with doubt in herself. *What could I have done better? How could have I misjudged who my husband truly was? How could he so easily betray me as well as everyone who loved him? Where did I go wrong? Could I have helped him more so he wouldn't have turned to drugs?*

The fact was that there was nothing Vanessa could have done to "fix" the situation or even to have prevented it. For longer than anyone could have imagined, her husband had been entrenched in deceit, theft, drugs and immorality—a world of darkness, living a double life. There was a side of him that no one knew or could know, because he had been so skilled at hiding his sins and being dishonest about them.

When we experience betrayal and hurt in our relationships, it is so tempting to allow our negative experiences to bleed into our relationships with Jesus. *Can I trust him? Does he really love me? Will he really forgive me? Will he keep his promises?* Jesus does not want us to compare him to or frame him by our earthly relationships. Our bond with him is distinct and special, and cannot be weighed or measured by our human associations. How can we overcome? Jesus says:

> *I have told you these things so you may have peace in Me. In the world you will have much trouble. But take hope! I have power over the world!*
> (John 16:33, NLV)

Jesus tells us that we can have peace in him. He knew we would have trouble in this world. When we do not have the strength or the drive to draw close to him, we just need to ask our Lord to draw close to us. He can give us hope when we have none, because Jesus overcame the world.

Vanessa ended up divorcing her husband, but her story did not end there. She decided to trust in Jesus and remain faithful to his plan for her life. She did not blame the Lord for her failed marriage. She did not become bitter toward her faith. She did not blame anyone for not seeing her husband's inadequacies and sins before they were married. Most of all, she did not lose hope and fall into self-pity. She decided to pray and to entrust herself to Jesus.

Though the years of "silence" to her prayers felt long, nine years later she met another man at church who swept her off her feet. They were married a short time afterward. They have since been blessed with a beautiful baby girl. Her new husband's last name is Mulligan, which in golf terms means a "do over." If there is a golf stroke that is considered a Mulligan, the new hole is recorded and scored as if the errant shot was never made. Vanessa feels like her husband, Joe, is her *Mulligan.* She feels wonderfully blessed by the Lord. She met someone who truly loves her. Her marriage now erases so much of the pain she experienced. It's as if the horrible incident never happened. She has truly received a "Mulligan" or a "do over" in Christ's grace.

God's grace is abounding. It is found in faith. It is nurtured through lordship and surrender. It continually cleanses us of the sins that keep overtaking us in this world, whether our own or those of others. It teaches us to say, "No" to the ungodliness of this world (Titus 2:12). It showers us with his love. And it proves how precious we truly are in our Lord's sight.

So whether you experience the goodness of Christ in your life like Miyoko, or you have faced terrible suffering like Vanessa, each of us is a bride of Christ. His grace is there in the good times and the bad times. His love is present in the greatest moments and the saddest moments. No matter what we have been through, he stands before the altar with his hand reaching out to us. He calls us to be with him forever as *his* bride, adorned with the purest white to wear, because we have remained steadfast in him, and his blood continually cleanses us.

> *Let us be glad and rejoice, and let us give honor to him. For the time has come for the wedding feast of the Lamb, and his bride has prepared herself. She has been given the finest of pure white linen to wear. For the fine linen represents the good deeds of God's holy people.*
>
> (Revelation 19:6-8, NLT)

 ## QUESTIONS FOR THE HEART

1. Read John 8:1-11 about the adulterous woman. And focus on how Jesus treated this woman.
2. Reflect on the ways that Jesus has shown you mercy this past year and write down at least two ways that you have seen his mercy through different circumstances.
3. Pray and thank Jesus for his mercy and love throughout the day today.

Chapter 11
MY FINAL THOUGHTS

In concluding this book on grace, how could I end it without mentioning a poem called "Footprints in the Sand," which has encouraged me through the years as a Christian? In this poem, Mary Stevenson writes about her journey through life. When she looks back at her life, she notices there are sometimes two set of footprints while at other times, the most difficult times, there is only one set of footprints in the sand. She says, "You promised me Lord, that if I followed you, you would walk with me always. But I have noticed that during the most trying periods of my life, there have only been one set of footprints in the sand." The Lord replies to her, "The times when you have seen only one set of footprints, is when I carried you."[13]

When each of us made a decision to make Jesus Lord of our lives, Jesus took us into his arms and began carrying us with his grace. There have been and will be times when we do not feel his arms carrying us, and there will only be "one set of footprints in the sand," which are deeper and more distinct, because he truly sustained us through those difficulties.

Sadly many of the memories of his grace can be erased by our lack of gratitude and by our focusing on those adverse times rather than on the ways that the Lord supported us through them. God wants us to look back at those different experiences and find *his* steps on the path. He doesn't want us find reasons to doubt him or to become bitter. We can, instead, find freedom when we choose not to linger on unhealthy thoughts, debilitating memories or unresolved disappointments (Philippians 4:8-9, NIV).

Though we may forget him, he never forgets us. He remembers us through the tough times. He remembers us when we call out to him. He remembers us when we try our best. He remembers us when we fail. He remembers us when we succeed. He remembers us when we are treated unfairly. He remembers us when we are all alone with no one who understands. Though he remembers us in all these ways, he chooses not remember our sins.

> *"For I will be merciful to their iniquities, and I will remember their sins no more."*
>
> (Hebrews 8:12, NASB)

We started this book with Adam and Eve. At the beginning of time, Eve had failed God by disobeying him. Eve was the impetus to bringing death into the world. She gave Adam the forbidden fruit, and he ate it. But God did not end his story for us women, there. God used another woman Mary, to bring grace into the world. Though a woman had broken faith with God, he did not hold it against her. In fact, he decided to use an imperfect woman to give birth to his perfect son and bring salvation to all of mankind.

I was in a pottery club in high school, where I learned to use the potter's wheel. Sometimes the clay did not take shape in the way I wanted, so my teacher would make me start over again. However, he would never let me throw away the clay. I had to reuse it by putting it back into a large pile of used clay, which he covered with a damp cloth to make it soft again. It did not matter how good you were at the potter's wheel, there were times when you had to start over.

In the same way, as God shapes us into the vessels we are meant to be, we might not become exactly the way he anticipated. But just like my pottery teacher, God will never throw us away. He will start over with us. This is his amazing grace. He will cover our sins and give us a "do over" when we make mistakes.

If this is how God treats us, how should we treat others?

There are people in all of our lives that need our grace. Since we live in an imperfect world as I have mentioned earlier, there will be many imperfect people who will cross our paths. Some of them, we will love no matter how much they mess up. In fact, we will love them more and more as the years go by. On the other hand, there will be others with whom we will have a hard time. They will irritate us and test our patience, making it hard for us to forgive them time and time again. Hopefully, seeing God's grace has given you a new hope and has planted in you a renewed motivation to show grace to others.

As I shared in the beginning of this book, my mother took her life, leaving my brother and me behind. I was angry and felt abandoned. I thought that she had loved me enough to persevere, even if it was hard for her. I had believed I was more important than her momentary troubles—important enough for her to live. But when I saw that my brother and I were not enough of a motivation for her, I was devastated. I had to forgive my mother. The letter that I wrote to her in the hotel room those many years ago contained words of thankfulness and *forgiveness*. One thing I do remember is that it had been subsequently eight years after my mother's death, and through those hours, I learned an important lesson about forgiveness. Grace towards others can release you from a prison of darkness. I am now free.

As the years go by and I grow older, I imagine and understand the pain and hopelessness my mother had probably felt. I also believe she, no doubt, felt trapped by the circumstances and the difficulties in her life. She never quite grasped the English language, so she did not have many friends to talk to. I know she had lost her father as a child, and, at the time, her own mother was very ill. She had recently lost her third child, which she did not want to talk about. She had also been suffering from lupus and, as a result, suffered with gangrene on both of her legs, so she took heavy doses of painkillers.

There were so many factors that, as woman in my early 20's, I could have never quite grasped, because I was too young. All I know is my mother had been enduring and suffering by herself. She had begun to go through menopause and did not know how to deal with some of those emotions. There were many aspects of her life I had not understood and known, including her history with depression. More than that, there was nothing more I could do about the four-month-old baby I was carrying in my womb, who I lost three days after my mother. In addition, I later discovered that I had the DNA for lupus, which took me to the very threshold of death just a few years later.

One thing I do know now as I look back at those chapters in my life is there is only one set of footsteps in the sand, which are *extra* deep. Not only had my Lord carried me, but he had also taken all my burdens upon himself. He showered me with "extra" grace during those stages of my life. I have learned when his grace took over in my heart, I was able to see life from God's perspective and not just my own, giving me the ability to loose the chains of my inner bondage.

What was God's perspective? I believe that through those afflictions, God gave me an "extraordinary" gift.

> *"Satan's angel did his best to get me down; what he in fact did was push me to my knees. No danger then of walking around high and mighty! At first I didn't think of it as a gift, and begged God to remove it. Three times I did that, and then he told me,*
>
> *My grace is enough; it's all you need. My strength comes into its own in your weakness.*
>
> *Once I heard that, I was glad to let it happen. I quit focusing on the handicap and began appreciating the gift. It was a case of Christ's strength moving in on my weakness. Now I take limitations in stride, and with good cheer, these limitations that cut me down to size—abuse, accidents, opposition, bad breaks. I just let Christ take over! And so the weaker I get, the stronger I become."*
>
> (2 Corinthians 12:8-10, The Message)

God gave me the grace of a remarkable tool to help others. With it, I, not only can sympathize with others, but I can truly *empathize* with them. He also gave me the ability in his *charis* to understand just a fraction of the torment my Jesus went through for my sins, which I can use as a powerful weapon against Satan. I am, therefore, driven to my knees to fight against my weaknesses. And I utilize my scars to keep me reliant on and close to my Lord.

This grace has allowed me to forgive myself. I am no longer held in captivity by a set of standards that changed my *daily* status in God's eyes. I no longer measure my salvation depending on my every action. I believed if a car ran over me at *the* moment I was thinking a bad thought, I would go to hell. I was plagued by thoughts like: *Did I do enough today that if I died, I could go to heaven? Did I live righteous enough today for God to be happy with me?* I have discovered a freedom in Christ where I no longer get down on myself constantly. It has also freed me from placing those chains on others in my life. God's grace has given me a capacity to be joyful, hopeful and faithful.

At the same time, in this flawed society, people will still measure us by our performance. How we look. How we act. How many results we have. In our effort to do our best, we are guaranteed to encounter bumps, judgmentalism and challenges, not just because of our flaws or because of other people but as a result of Satan's schemes. He wants nothing more than for us to forget God's grace and to reject his love, because he knows how powerful it is.

God's grace and love are what defeated the Devil on the cross. And they are what will continue to overturn all his evil plans, if we cling to his promises. The world belongs to the evil one; therefore, there is very little grace. There are societies I have lived in, like Japan, where the concept of grace is non-existent. For instance, once you have claimed bankruptcy, you can never have a bank account or credit card ever again. If you fail that one entrance exam, you cannot take it over again. Mistakes are not tolerated in that country in any shape or form.

Dear sisters, wherever you live, even if *your* world is ungracious, you do not need to be controlled by it. God's grace is always before you and is available to you. Remember that you are precious, valuable and loved. You do not have to prove yourself to God. He will accept you and love you as you are. Just like Mary, the mother of Jesus, you do not have to prove yourself to be chosen by God. As a matter of fact, she had never been a mother before. There was no past experience to base her "credentials" on. When we consider this, we see God's grace is all about God and not about our perfection. Let us leave the perfection part up to him.

What about our weaknesses? What about all our failures? Hopefully, you will stop trying to prove yourself worthy before God and judge yourself less harshly. Then, you will be compelled to change into a confident woman who sees the reality of your beauty as God sees it.

> *So too, at the present time there is a remnant chosen by grace. And if by grace, then it is no longer by works; if it were, grace would no longer be grace.*
>
> (Romans 11:5-6, NIV)

Even Jesus was weak and tempted by sin. Now Jesus sits on a throne of grace. He pours out his mercy on you and me, though we don't deserve it. Through him, we can find the strength and the help that we need, because he can also sympathize with us—with *our* weaknesses. Jesus is amazing!

In the end, we will someday be sitting beside him on that throne of grace, knowing that we are not worthy to be there. He will hold our hands and encourage us by saying, "You are my good and faithful friend and servant." And as he says these words, we will wonder what he means by those words. Inside our minds, we will remember our lies, our selfishness, our lust, our greed, our anger, and not to mention all the other myriad of sins we do not even recall, then wonder why we would merit such a high compliment from our Lord. Then Jesus, knowing what we are thinking, will say, "It's not about you, my dear sweet daughter. Your perfection is not what got you here. It's all about our special relationship. Besides, I know that through it all—your struggles, your sins and your weaknesses—you always turned back to me. You kept your eyes on the cross and kept believing in me!"

Most of all, when we look at God's Word, we will no longer see a "rule book" that tells us the guidelines of how to be a "good" person or tells us all the ways we are not good enough. We will read it, learn from it and mature through it during our lifetime, because it's God's love letters to us. It took him centuries upon centuries to bring it to completion. He wants us to know his Word and to be strengthened by it. He wants it to be a light in this darkness.

So the Word became human and made his home among us. He was full of unfailing love and faithfulness. And we have seen his glory, the glory of the Father's one and only Son.

(John 1:14, NLT)

Likewise, we have the living Word, Jesus, walking with us, beside us and within us. When we see his grace, we will also see his glory.

I have seen the glory Christ through the gift of certain people in my life, who have "made up" for some of the loss I have felt. The first couple to "adopt" me as a daughter was George and Irene Gurganus. Irene was there for me as I grieved over my mother. She took me in and loved me through the loss of my babies as well. When my second and third daughters were born, Irene was the first woman other than me to hold my babies and to greet them into this world. When my brother died, Irene held me tight once again and let me wet her shoulders with my tears. I returned the "favor," when George was dying. I was beside Irene for the last three weeks, crying with her and praying with her until her husband passed away. A few days before Irene passed away, I was able to visit her for the last time and reminisce about our lives together.

After Irene died, God provided me with Al and Gloria Baird who have been parents to me through some of the most difficult times as well. They have provided me with wisdom and healing through my later years. They have been there to watch my daughters grow up and get married. They have stood by us and supported us through our career and life changes. Their friendship and times of laughing, crying and rejoicing have sustained me. Every year, we go away with them on vacation. Each of those occasions has been a source of encouragement and inspiration for my faith. Recently, they sat right next to me, in the place of my parents, at the weddings of each of my daughters, to rejoice with me and to fill in the gap, because I had no immediate family at my daughters' weddings. Al and Gloria are truly family to me, and I know that I am family to them.

Most of all, God has shown me grace through my husband Frank, who has loved me through all the many years of adversity and pain. My immediate family is gone, and I feel like an orphan. But Frank has been there for me and has held me in his arms, lending me his shoulder to cry on, trying to make up for all the loss I have felt. Of course, he cannot replace those I have lost, but he tries his best to love me in place of my grandparents, parents and brother.

I look back at every step of my life, and I feel the healing hand of God through these people my God has provided. I clearly see the footprints in the sand where I had only seen pain and tragedy beforehand. For me, I now realize it was never about me, but it was all about God's grace all along.

I am confident that his gracious hand will cover whatever I have been lacking or will lack in the future. His grace is truly sufficient. His power is truly made perfect in *my* weaknesses and *my* shortcomings. In all of this, I have *felt* God's love for me.

> *"This is how much God loved the world: He gave his Son, his one and only Son. And this is why: so that no one need be destroyed; by believing in him, anyone can have a whole and lasting life. God didn't go to all the trouble of sending his Son merely to point an accusing finger, telling the world how bad it was. He came to help, to put the world right again. Anyone who trusts in him is acquitted; anyone who refuses to trust him has long since been under the death sentence without knowing it. And why? Because of that person's failure to believe in the one-of-a-kind Son of God when introduced to him."*
>
> (John 3:16-18, The Message)

I do not profess to be an expert on God's grace by any means, nor do I believe I have some sort of exceptional faith. I also am not claiming to have a special "in" with the Lord in any way. But I believe that God has shown me his grace abundantly, and I have wanted to share this good news with each one of you. My life has been far from perfect, and I have learned to rely on my perfect God to carry me through the times when I have fallen short. Maybe, some of my experiences reflect certain times in your life you can relate with. Wherever you are at in your walk with the Lord, I pray that these pages have been a blessing to you.

Hopefully, you can see a little more of the grace God has for you, ready to be poured out and to be lavished on you. We cannot truly comprehend all of it to its fullest extent, with it being so magnificent and far-reaching. While it is the key to our salvation, the portal to God's heavenly kingdom, and the gift of everlasting life, his grace gives us so much more. No one but a person who has tasted heaven for a brief moment can ever appreciate even a fraction of this amazing and precious blessing we have been given.

What does God want from us in return for all of this? He wants us to stand firm and allow nothing to move us.

> *With all this going for us, my dear, dear friends, stand your ground. And don't hold back. Throw yourselves into the work of the Master, confident that nothing you do for him is a waste of time or effort.*
>
> (1 Corinthians 15:58, The Message)

Most of all, he wants us to grow in his grace. Will we be tempted to sin over and over again? Of course we will. Will we fall into sin? Sadly, yes. Will there be people along the way who hurt us deeply? There probably will. Will we be able to correct all the injustices of this world in the process? We probably will never be able to change this world. Will we ever achieve being a perfect Christian? Not until the final trumpet sounds from heaven, and we are changed will we be able to conquer our flesh.

> *Therefore, since we have been justified through faith, we have peace with God through our Lord Jesus Christ, through whom we have gained access by faith into this grace in which we now stand. And we rejoice in the hope of the glory of God.*
>
> (Romans 5:1-2, NIV)

Dear sisters, I pray you will continue to find his footprints in the sand through your walk with the Lord—whether long or short. And at the end of your life, Lord willing, you will see and know with absolute confidence that it was only his grace that carried you all the way home… *Through many dangers, toils and snares I have already come; 'Tis Grace that brought me safe thus far and Grace will lead me home.* Let his patient and enduring love bring you all the way home!

FOOTNOTES

1. http://www.dailymail.co.uk/news/article-2369218/Worlds-oldest-mother-Rajo-Devi-Lohan-74-says-giving-birth-daughter-kept-living-longer.html

2. Koenig, Harold G. and Fernando A. Lucchese Religion, spirituality and cardiovascular disease: research, clinical implications, and opportunities in Brazil, Rev Bras Cir Cardiovasc vol.28 no.1 São José do Rio Preto Jan./Mar. 2013

3. http://en.wikipedia.org/wiki/Yoke

4. Added "woman's" for emphasis

5. A statement of 1877, as quoted in *From Telegraph to Light Bulb with Thomas Edison* (2007) by Deborah Hedstrom, p. 22

6. As quoted in an ad for GPU Nuclear Corporation, in *Black Enterprise* Vol. 16, No. 11 (June 1986), p. 79

7. http://www.goodreads.com/author/quotes/3091287.Thomas_Edison

8. E. Meyers & J. Strange, *Archaeology, the Rabbis, & Early Christianity* Nashville: Abingdon, 1981; Article "Nazareth" in the *Anchor Bible Dictionary.* New York: Doubleday, 1992.

9. http://www.bibletools.org/index.cfm/fuseaction/Topical.show/RTD/cgg/ID/2704/Worship-Mary.htm

10. http://biblesuite.com/greek/3107.htm

11. http://www.cgg.org/index.cfm/fuseaction/Audio.details/ID/584/A-Survey-Gods-Gifts-Us.htm

12. http://www.nist.gov/el/disasterstudies/earthquake/earthquake_kobe_japan1995.cfm

13. http://www.footprints-inthe-sand.com/index.php?page=Poem/Poem.php

CPSIA information can be obtained at www.ICGtesting.com
Printed in the USA
BVOW05*1146050615

403396BV00011B/183/P